OUVERTURE

Cadences   Livre 3
Vivre en collectivité

L120 course team

OU team

Ghislaine Adams (*course manager*)
Marie-Claude Bovet (*course secretary*)
Joan Carty *(liaison librarian)*
Ann Cobbold (*course secretary*)
Jonathan Davies (*design group co-ordinator*)
Tony Duggan (*project controller*)
Jane Duffield (*project controller*)
Kevin Firth (*team member/author*)
Janis Gilbert (*graphic artist*)
David Hare (*team member/author*)
Pam Higgins (*designer*)
Angela Jamieson (*BBC producer*)
Marie-Noëlle Lamy (*course team chair/author*)
Kate Laughton (*editor*)
Mike Levers (*photographer*)
Ruth McCracken (*course manager*)
Reginald Melton *(IET)*
Hélène Mulphin (*team member/author*)
Jenny Ollerenshaw (*team member/author*)
Margaret Selby (*course secretary*)
Anne Stevens (*reading member*)
Betty Talks (*BBC series producer*)
Penny Vine (*BBC producer*)

External assessor

Professor Samuel Taylor (Department of French, University of St Andrews)

External consultants

Authors who contributed to the writing of the materials were: Martyn Bird; Elspeth Broady; Lucile Ducroquet; Brigitte Guénier; Philip Handley; Rod Hares; Hélène Lewis; Margaret Mitchell; Sandra Truscott; Margaret Tuccori.

Critical readers were: Lucette Barbarin; Malcolm Bower; Brian Page; John Pettit; Pam Shakespeare; Richard Tuffs. Bob Powell was the language adviser.

Supplementary picture and text research by Pierrick Picot. Proofs read by Danièle Bourdais.

Developmental testing

The course team would like to thank all those people involved in testing the course materials. Their comments have been invaluable in the preparation of the course. In particular, thanks go to the following members of IET: Beryl Crooks; Ellie Chambers; Barbara Hodgson; Reginald Melton; Kay Pole; Don Whitehead; Alan Woodley; Hussein Zand.

The team would also like to thank the following adult education tutors: Liz Moss; Adèle Skegg; Theresa Young.

The Open University, Walton Hall, Milton Keynes MK7 6AA

First published 1994. Reprinted 1996; 1997

Edited, designed and typeset by the Open University

Printed in the United Kingdom by Butler and Tanner

ISBN 0 7492 6285 0

This text forms part of an Open University course. If you would like a copy of *Studying with the Open University* or more information on Open University language materials, please write to the Course Enquiries Data Service, P.O. Box 625, The Open University, Dane Road, Milton Keynes MK1 1TY.

Contents

Introduction

In this book we visit four different institutions where, either by choice or not, people live a communal life. Section 1, *À l'internat*, is set in a girls' boarding school, Section 2, *À l'armée*, looks at life in a military barracks and Section 3, *À la prison*, deals with a women's prison. The final section, *Au monastère*, looks at what life is like in a Trappist monastery and gives you chance to watch a more extended video sequence. This section is optional. The common themes running through the book are the constraints and restrictions communal life imposes on members of the communities, but also the advantages that such a life can bring.

The main grammar associated with this book relates to the use of past tenses. Also, as you discover what members of the various communities like and dislike about their life styles and what they are allowed and forbidden to do by the rules of their institutions, you'll learn how to express your own likes and dislikes and to talk about obligation.

The Feature Cassette that accompanies this book is set in the prison. You can listen to it at any point, but it would probably be most helpful to do so as you are working through the material in Section 3.

1 À l'internat

STUDY CHART

	Topic	Activity/timing	Audio/video	Key points
2 hrs 25 mins	1.1 Une journée à Blanche de Castille	1 (10 mins)	Audio	Recognizing *il faut* when it is used to say what people must do
		2 (5 mins)	Audio	Using *il faut* to say what you must do
		3 (20 mins)	Audio	
		4 (20 mins)		Understanding *en* + present participle
		5 (10 mins)	Audio	Vocabulary: boarding school routine
		6 (15 mins)	Audio	Recognizing phrases for what you're allowed and not allowed to do
		7 (15 mins)		Using phrases for what you're allowed and not allowed to do
		8 (20 mins)		Understanding regulations
2 hrs 20 mins	1.2 Contraintes et avantages	9 (10 mins)	Audio	Recognizing phrases for what you must and must not do
		10 (20 mins)		Using phrases for what you must and must not do
		11 (10 mins)	Audio	Talking about likes and dislikes
		12 (15 mins)	Audio	
		13 (15 mins)	Audio	
		14 (10 mins)		Vocabulary: school life. Talking about advantages
		15 (15 mins)	Audio	
		16 (15 mins)		Talking about change using *plus … plus, moins … moins*
		17 (5 mins)	Audio	Using *en* + present participle

Topic	Activity/timing	Audio/video	Key points
1.3 *Pension prison*	18 (20 mins)		Secondary education in France
	19 (15 mins)	Audio	Hearing and pronouncing the difference between [ə] and [ɛ]
	20 (20 mins)	Audio	Vocabulary: doing badly at school
	21 (20 mins)	Audio	Distinguishing aurally between the perfect and imperfect tenses
	22 (15 mins)		Understanding the distinction between perfect and imperfect tenses

1 hr 30 mins

In this section you will be hearing about life for the girls in the Institution Blanche de Castille, a Catholic boarding school near Nantes. You will work primarily with extracts from audio interviews with Fabienne and Anne-Catherine, two of the boarders there. In the first topic, *Une journée à Blanche de Castille*, they talk about their daily routine and some of the regulations they have to abide by. Then, in *Contraintes et avantages*, they discuss the advantages and disadvantages of their carefully structured life: for example, the close friendships on the one hand, and the restrictions on the other. Finally, in *Pension prison*, you'll learn a little more about the French school system and find out why girls like Anne-Catherine are sent to private schools like Blanche de Castille.

As you work through the section, you'll revise times and numbers and study the kinds of expression used to talk about obligation and restrictions. You'll also look at how the perfect and the imperfect tenses are used to recount past experiences.

1.1 Une journée à Blanche de Castille

In the first two audio extracts in this section Fabienne and Anne-Catherine describe the daily routine at Blanche de Castille. You will be working on this recording in two parts: *Le matin* and then *L'après-midi et le soir*.

Le matin

In the first audio extract Fabienne describes how the boarders at Blanche de Castille get woken up by a nun (*une sœur*) who goes along the corridors calling out '*Levez-vous! Il est l'heure!*' As you will hear, the rest of the morning is then very much ordered by a bell (*une sonnerie*). Fabienne uses

Fabienne   **Anne-Catherine**

the expression *il faut* followed by a verb in the infinitive to talk about what the girls have to do. In *Activité 1* you will need to listen for this structure, while *Activités 2* and *3* provide you with an opportunity to practise it yourself.

Activité 1
10 MINUTES
AUDIO 1

Look at the table below and then listen to the audio extract, paying particular attention to the times that are mentioned in order to identify what the girls have to do when. Remember: there are different ways of stating times and you need to be alert to how they are expressed on the cassette and in the table. As you are listening, fill in the details missing from the table.

Écoutez Fabienne et remplissez la grille ci-dessous. Attention à la manière d'indiquer les horaires: la cassette et la grille diffèrent.

Heure	*Qu'est-ce qu'il faut faire?*
À 7 : 2 0	il faut se réveiller
À sept heures cinquante	il faut *descendre*
À 8 30	il faut aller au premier cours
À douze heures vingt-cinq	il faut *déjeuner*

Pour vous aider

qui nous prévient que   which tells us that
éviter   to avoid

4

Expressing obligation: 'il faut' + infinitive and 'devoir'

As you have just heard, the expression *il faut* + infinitive is a useful one for talking about what has to be done. This construction is impersonal, that is, it can be used only in the *il* form. It tends therefore to be used to express a general obligation. If, however, you want to specify who has to do something, you can use the verb *devoir* (see your Grammar Book, page 167, for its conjugation). For example, if you say *'je dois faire la vaisselle'*, then you can be certain nobody else will volunteer for the washing-up! *'Il faut faire la vaisselle'*, on the other hand, could imply that (a) the washing-up needs doing and you might do it, or (b) you want somebody else to do it.

In the next two *activités* you will practise using *il faut* + infinitive to talk about what needs to be done.

Activité 2
5   MINUTES
A U D I O   2

You are discussing plans for a day out in London with a French friend. Listen to the English prompts on the audio extract and reply accordingly in French using *il faut* + infinitive.

Répondez aux questions en utilisant l'expression 'il faut' + infinitif.

Activité 3
2 0   MINUTES
A U D I O   3

You are about to leave the gîte where you have been staying for a week. Read the following list, which is pinned up on the kitchen wall, and then in Audio Extract 3 answer your friend's questions about what has to be done in the kitchen before you leave. Use *il faut* + infinitive.

Lisez la liste suivante, puis répondez aux questions en utilisant l'expression 'il faut' + infinitif.

```
     POUR UN BON SÉJOUR  -  RÈGLES À SUIVRE
               Avant de partir...
  -    nettoyer
  -    vider la poubelle
  -    éteindre le frigo
  -    prendre note du numéro du compteur
       électrique
  -    mettre les serviettes sales dans le
       panier à linge
  -    faire l'inventaire
  -    avertir le propriétaire de votre départ
```

'En' + present participle

Now we move on to look at a construction that Fabienne used in her account of the morning routine. Look at the following sentences taken from Audio Extract 1:

> Nous sommes réveillées… par la sœur qui passe dans le couloir **en frappant** dans ses mains, **en** nous **disant** 'Levez-vous, il est l'heure!'

> … on part tous* **en courant**, euh, vers la cantine pour éviter de faire la queue.

> (* she should have said *'toutes'*)

En + present participle (*disant, courant,* etc.) is a construction which can be used to give more information about the main action, often telling us how that action is performed and what is going on at the same time. So, in the first sentence above, we learn that the boarders are woken by a nun who goes along the corridor, simultaneously clapping her hands and calling out 'It's time to get up!' Similarly, in the second sentence, the *en courant* tells us that the girls go running off to the canteen.

Forming present participles

Frappant, disant and *courant* are all forms of the verb known as the present participle. It is formed by taking the *nous* form of the verb, removing the *-ons* ending and adding *-ant*.

> nous frappons → frapp + ant → frappant

> nous finissons → finiss + ant → finissant

> nous vendons → vend + ant → vendant

Verbs ending in *-ger* and *-cer* make slight changes in the *nous* form of the verb to maintain the soft [ʒ] and [s] pronunciations which occur only when the letters 'g' and 'c' come before an 'e' or an 'i'. For example:

> nous mang**e**ons, nous annon**ç**ons

The additional 'e' and the change of 'c' to 'ç' are also found in the present participles of these verbs:

> mangeant, annonçant

Irregular present participles

Note the following exceptions to the pattern above:

> avoir → ayant   être → étant   savoir → sachant

Now you're aware of the present participle, you'll probably notice quite a few examples of it in this book. You might like to make a note of some of them in your dossier. You will find more information about the present participle on pages 145–6 of the Grammar Book.

We'll be returning to look at the use of this construction in more detail later on in this section, but first try your hand at *Activité 4*. In Book 2 of *Cadences* you looked at the daily routine of various working people. In the following *activité*, someone with a bit more time on her hands describes how she spends the early summer mornings watching the comings and goings in her street.

Activité 4
20 MINUTES

1   Fill in the gaps in the following text with *en* + the present participle of an appropriate verb. You'll find the missing phrases in the box.

Choisissez dans l'encadré les expressions qui conviennent pour compléter ce texte.

Souvent l'été, je me lève très tôt et je prends mon petit déjeuner sur le balcon _____ _____ ce qui se passe dans ma rue. Vers sept heures, j'entends le facteur qui descend la rue _____ _____ . Heureusement qu'il a une belle voix! Quand il passe devant ma fenêtre, il me donne mon courrier _____ _____ _____ 'Encore des lettres d'amour pour vous, Mademoiselle Fournier?' Ensuite, je vois mon voisin, Monsieur Prost, qui part _____ _____ vers la gare. Il est toujours en retard! Il oublie toujours quelque chose. Et puis vers huit heures moins dix, j'entends des portes claquer. Ce sont les enfants qui partent à l'école _____ _____ et _____ _____ _____ , leur cartable sur le dos.

> en criant, en regardant, en chantant,
> en me disant, en courant, en se bousculant

Pour vous aider

se bousculant   jostling one another
leur cartable sur le dos   with their school bags on their backs

2   Read through the completed text and jot down a rough translation of it, concentrating on how you would translate the *en* + present participle constructions into English.

Traduisez le texte ci-dessus et faites attention à la façon de traduire 'en' + participe présent.

L'après-midi et le soir

In the next audio extract Fabienne and Anne-Catherine describe the afternoon and evening routine at Blanche de Castille. Anne-Catherine explains in particular what happens during private study time (*l'étude*). She also mentions the rules and regulations (*le règlement*) at Blanche de Castille which govern, among other things, when the girls can visit each other. Fabienne then talks about what happens after private study time. *Activité 5* will help you understand what the girls say, then in *Activité 6* you will focus on expressions used to talk about what is and is not allowed.

Activité 5

10 MINUTES

AUDIO 4

1 To understand the general meaning of this audio extract, try to establish the sequence of events which make up the afternoon and evening routine. Look at the lists below and as you listen pay particular attention to the time phrases listed on the left and match them up with the correct activity listed on the right. Not every phrase is a literal transcription of what the girls say. You need to work out some of the answers yourself on the basis of the information they give.

Écoutez l'extrait en faisant attention aux expressions de temps données à gauche. Regardez ensuite à droite et indiquez pour chacune l'activité correspondante.

(a) Après le déjeuner,

(b) Ensuite,

(c) Après l'étude, à sept heures quinze,

(d) En général, à huit heures moins le quart,

(e) Entre sept heures quarante-cinq et neuf heures,

(i) nous pouvons écouter de la musique.

(ii) nous remontons dans nos chambres.

(iii) nous avons les cours normaux de l'après-midi et une petite récréation.

(iv) nous avons l'étude.

(v) nous allons dîner.

Pour vous aider

une petite récréation a short break

surveillée supervised

chacune d'entre nous each one of us

aller les unes chez les autres to visit each other's rooms

ça les empêche de travailler it stops them from working

2 Listen to the audio extract again and answer the following questions briefly in French.

Écoutez encore une fois cet extrait et répondez aux questions suivantes en français.

(a) Pendant l'une des deux périodes non surveillées, les jeunes filles doivent travailler: est-ce avant ou après le dîner?

(b) Que font-elles pendant l'autre période non surveillée?

As you have just discovered, the rules at Blanche de Castille forbid boarders from going to each other's rooms during the private study period when they are supposed to be working. However, they are allowed to get together after dinner. Fabienne and Anne-Catherine use two very useful constructions in this audio extract to indicate what is forbidden and what is allowed.

Activité 6

15 MINUTES

AUDIO 4

Listen to Audio Extract 4 again and fill in the missing words.

Réécoutez l'extrait et trouvez les mots qui manquent.

> Ensuite nous avons l'étude qui n'est pas surveillée, c'est-à-dire que chacune d'entre nous reste dans sa chambre, pour travailler; mais, euh…, donc _____ _____ d'aller les unes chez les autres car ça les empêche de travailler.
>
> En général, à huit heures moins le quart nous avons terminé de dîner, nous remontons dans nos chambres et… et là _____ _____ _____ _____ d'aller chacune les unes chez les autres.

Stating what you must and must not do

'C'est interdit de' + infinitive

You heard Anne-Catherine use the above phrase in the previous audio extract. Literally translated, it means 'it is forbidden to'. (In more formal contexts you will also hear *il est interdit de*.) Note that this construction, like *il faut*, is an impersonal one and is used only in the *il* (or the *ce*) form. Lists of other impersonal verbs are on pages 113–16 in your Grammar Book.

You can also use *interdit* as an adjective. For example, the French translation of 'No parking' is *Stationnement interdit,* while 'No entry' is *Entrée interdite*.

Note also the following examples where *interdit* is used with the verb *être*:

> *Les radios sont interdites sur la plage.*
> Radios are not allowed on the beach.

'On a le droit de' + infinitive

Literally, *on a le droit de* means 'we have (or one has) the right to'. Note that *avoir le droit de* is not an impersonal verb. Fabienne uses it in the *on* form,

Il y a pas mal de choses qui sont interdites sur cette plage!

meaning 'we are allowed' (see Book 1 of *Cadences* for a reminder of how to use *on*). If you were talking about what you yourself were allowed to do, you would say *j'ai le droit de*.

The next *activité* provides you with immediate practice of these structures by asking you to identify some of the rules and restrictions that apply to everyday situations in France and Great Britain. There will be other *activités* later in this book where you can consolidate your command of these structures.

Activité 7
1 5   M I N U T E S

Complete the following sentences in French, taking your cue from the pictures below. You should use the appropriate form of one of the structures we have just looked at: *avoir le droit de* + infinitive, *il est interdit de* + infinitive, or *être interdit*.

Complétez les phrases suivantes en français d'après les illustrations ci-dessous en utilisant les structures que vous venez d'étudier.

1   Dans les cinémas en Grande-Bretagne et en France, vous n'avez…

2   Dans beaucoup de musées français, il…

3   Dans beaucoup de forêts françaises, le camping…

4   En Grande-Bretagne, les commerces…

**OPEN
SUNDAYS
9-5**

5   Dans les pubs anglais, seules les personnes de plus de dix-huit ans…

**NO
UNDER
18s**

6   Sur beaucoup de plages en France, les chiens…

en passant » » » »

Most European road signs have now been standardized, but have you ever seen this sign in a French street and wondered what it meant? The explanation is in French below.

Ce panneau indique que vous avez le droit de garer votre voiture d'un côté de la rue du 1 au 15 du mois, et de l'autre côté du 16 au 31 du mois!

» » » »

La vie à l'internat

We now go back to Blanche de Castille to find out a little more about the routine and regulations there, this time comparing what Fabienne and Anne-Catherine have said with information presented in the written text *La vie à l'internat*. This text is a handout for new entrants to the school and it was written several months after the interviews with the two *pensionnaires* were recorded.

As you read, you'll come across a number of verbs in the future tense: *essaiera* from *essayer*, *vivrons* from *vivre*, *auras* from *avoir* and *pourras* from *pouvoir*. We don't expect you to learn the future tense at this stage (you already know how to talk about future events by using *aller* + infinitive, see Book 1 of *Cadences*). However, if you would like more information on the future tense, look at page 93 of your Grammar Book.

Activité 8
20 MINUTES

1   Read through the *La vie à l'internat* text and try to spot any discrepancies between the information contained there and what you already know about the school's routine from the recordings of Fabienne and Anne-Catherine. If necessary, listen to Audio Extracts 1 and 4 again and go through your notes. Then write down the differences you find in French: there are five in total. You'll find the expression *selon* meaning 'according to' will be useful. Here is an example of what you might write:

> Selon Fabienne et Anne-Catherine, les jeunes filles sont réveillées à sept heures vingt. Selon le texte, elles sont réveillées à sept heures quinze.

> *Lisez le texte et comparez les détails de la routine quotidienne avec les explications de Fabienne et d'Anne-Catherine. Notez en français les différences que vous trouvez.*

VIE A L'INTERNAT

Tu es la bienvenue à l'internat et chacun essaiera de te rendre la vie agréable.

Néanmoins il est nécessaire que tu sois bien au courant de la façon dont nous vivrons ensemble pour que cette vie soit facile, joyeuse et riche pour tous.

Voici le programme de tes journées :

7 H 15 Réveil...
Tu fais ta toilette, ton lit, tu ranges ta chambre et tu descends au petit déjeuner vers...

7 H 45 Tu auras au choix: café, thé, chocolat, lait, avec pain, beurre et confiture, on te donne un biscuit pour la récréation. Puis tu quittes l'internat à partir de...

8 H 10 Tu rejoins ta classe, n'oublie pas tes affaires!...

TU NE POURRAS EN AUCUN CAS REMONTER AU DORTOIR APRES 8 H.

16 H 45 Tu fais ton cartable et quittes l'externat avant 17 H.
Goûter. Avec un ticket tu peux te procurer pain, chocolat ou pâte de fruits. Tu peux te détendre... sur la terrasse et le terrain de sports devant le château.

17 H 15 Tu vas travailler en permanence.
Pendant le temps de travail, le SILENCE TOTAL EST EXIGE. Aucun déplacement n'est permis. Si des élèves veulent travailler ensemble, elles pourront le faire à la pause et après le dîner.

19 H 20 Début du self 4è-3è.
Les 4è et 3è qui veulent travailler après le repas emportent leurs affaires. Le collège sera fermé après 19 H. Le cuisinier et ses aides soignent particulièrement les menus. Alors, sois polie et pense à remercier. Ne traîne pas pour te rendre au réfectoire.

APRES LE REPAS

Les dortoirs sont ouverts à 20 H : pour te reposer, pour lire ou pour travailler (3è), toujours en SILENCE.

Tu pourras sortir sur la terrasse s'il fait jour, rester dans les réfectoires, ou te rendre au foyer pour voir les informations à la télévision.
Une fois par semaine tu auras la possibilité de voir une émission télévisée en direct ou en vidéo choisie dès le lundi.
Tu peux aussi travailler seule ou avec d'autres.

A 21 H Toutes doivent être au dortoir.

21 H 30 Extinction des lumières.

Pour vous aider

tu es la bienvenue welcome

que tu sois bien au courant de that you should be well informed about

pour que cette vie soit so that this life should be

tu rejoins ta classe you go to the classroom

en aucun cas in no circumstances

l'externat the teaching block (where day pupils and boarders are during the day)

tu peux te procurer you can obtain

en permanence in the supervised study room

aucun déplacement n'est permis it is strictly forbidden to move about

début du self cafeteria opens (*le self* is *le restaurant self-service*)

au foyer in the pupils' common room (more commonly, a *foyer* is a residential block used by the pupils of a school, the workers of a factory, etc.)

2 The *Vie à l'internat* text contains some expressions for talking about everyday activities which will be useful to you later on. Identify them by looking for the French equivalents of the following English expressions.

Trouvez dans le texte les expressions françaises qui traduisent les expressions anglaises suivantes.

(a) You get washed.

(b) You tidy up your room.

(c) Don't forget your things.

(d) You can relax.

(e) To watch the news on television.

1.2 Contraintes et avantages

In this topic the girls talk about the advantages and disadvantages of being at boarding school. Obviously, there are quite a lot of restrictions (*des contraintes*) to life in such a school, as you will have gathered from the set of rules you've just read. This is confirmed by Fabienne in the next audio extract. However, there is also a positive side to Blanche de Castille, which comes over very clearly in comments written by one of the boarders and in Anne-Catherine and Fabienne's discussion of the advantages of their private education at the school.

Les contraintes

In the next audio extract Fabienne identifies three *contraintes*. She uses two constructions to express these restrictions: *on (ne) peut pas* + infinitive (note that she barely sounds the 'n') and *on est obligé de* + infinitive. Note, too, that we have added the feminine plural ending *-es* to *obligées* in the next *activité*. This is because Fabienne is referring here to herself and the other girls.

Activité 9

10 MINUTES

Listen to the audio extract and fill in the gaps in the following sentences with what Fabienne says.

Écoutez Fabienne et remplissez les trous avec les mots qui manquent.

On (ne) peut pas:

1 _____ _____ _____ aussi souvent que chez soi.

2 _____ _____ _____ _____ tard le soir, lire donc très longtemps.

On est obligé(es) de:

3 _____ aux autres.

You have now met several constructions which can be used to express what is allowed and what is not allowed, what you may and may not do, and what you have to do. Given what you already know about Blanche de Castille, what other things are likely to be allowed or not allowed? In the next *activité* we want you to make sentences about other likely rules, using the structures you have looked at so far.

Activité 10
20 MINUTES

1 In the list below choose which construction you need to make a meaningful sentence.

Dans chacune des phrases suivantes, choisissez la construction qui convient.

(a) Il est interdit d'/On est obligé(e) d'écouter de la musique après vingt et une heures.

(b) On doit/On ne peut pas laisser la lumière allumée après vingt et une heures trente.

(c) Il ne faut pas/On doit courir dans les couloirs.

(d) On est obligé(e) de/On a le droit de se lever à sept heures vingt.

(e) On doit/On n'est pas obligé(e) de travailler en silence pendant l'étude.

(f) On a le droit de/On est obligé(e) de regarder la télévision une fois par semaine.

2 Now make up some sentences about constraints and obligations you experience in your own life, using each of the constructions listed below. You don't have to start with the expression given, but you can build up your sentence around it, as in the following example:

À midi, **je suis obligé(e)** de manger dans un restaurant, parce qu'il n'y a pas de cantine là où je travaille.

Maintenant inventez vos propres phrases en utilisant chacune des structures suivantes.

(a) Je suis obligé(e) de.

(b) Je n'ai pas le droit de.

(c) Il est interdit de.

(d) Je ne peux pas.

(e) Je dois.

Now let's go back to Fabienne's comments on the restrictions at Blanche de Castille. She emphasizes the *contraintes*, but is it your impression that she is happy there or not?

Activité 11

10 MINUTES

AUDIO 5

In the list below tick the two general comments Fabienne makes about life at the school. You'll probably need to listen again to Audio Extract 5.

Cochez dans la liste suivante les deux commentaires que fait Fabienne sur la vie à Blanche de Castille. Si c'est nécessaire, réécoutez l'Extrait 5 pour vérifier.

1   *C'est très difficile.*   It's very difficult.   ❑

2   *Ça me plaît beaucoup.*   I like it a lot.   ❑

3   *C'est insupportable.*   It's unbearable/I can't stand it.   ❑

4   *C'est facile.*   It's easy.   ❑

5   *Ça ne me plaît pas du tout.*   I don't like it at all.   ❑

6   *C'est supportable.*   It's bearable/tolerable.   ❑

Comments such as those listed in *Activité 11* are very useful for increasing your conversational fluency. The next *activité* will help you memorize them and then in *Activité 13* you'll practise using them in a dialogue.

Activité 12

15 MINUTES

AUDIO 6

For pronunciation practice, listen to the audio extract and repeat the phrases in the gaps that have been left.

Écoutez la prononciation des phrases suivantes et répétez-les dans les pauses.

- C'est très difficile.
- Ça me plaît beaucoup.
- C'est insupportable.
- C'est facile.
- Ça ne me plaît pas du tout.
- C'est supportable.

Activité 13

15 MINUTES

AUDIO 7

In this audio extract you are discussing with a French friend your new job in London and the problems of commuting. You will hear prompts in English and you should answer using phrases from the list in *Activité 12*.

Répondez aux questions sur votre cassette. Écoutez les suggestions en anglais et utilisez les phrases que vous venez d'apprendre.

Les avantages

We now look at the advantages of being at Blanche de Castille. We asked one of the boarders to write down her comments on the school. As you will see, in general she is very positive about it. The vocabulary in this text is fairly straightforward and there are expressions here which you will find useful.

Activité 14
10 MINUTES

1 Read the text, then look at statements (a)–(d) on the next page. They summarize the main points in English. Beside each statement note down the numbers of the corresponding point or points from the French text.

Lisez le texte ci-dessous et les phrases (a)–(d) qui suivent. À côté des phrases anglaises, notez le numéro qui correspond à chaque description française.

1. Les professeurs sont assez motivants, ils s'intéressent à nous et à nos problèmes (scolaires ou familiaux).

2. C'est un établissement assez moderne avec des ordinateurs, un labo de langues et une grande salle de sport.

3. L'ambiance n'est pas toujours très bonne entre filles (il n'y a pas assez de garçons).

4. Il y a beaucoup de sorties et de voyages culturels et linguistiques.

5. Les professeurs sont rarement absents.

6. Cadre agréable avec un grand parc.

7. École dynamique car elle participe à des concours et organise des activités sportives.

8. Les responsables de l'établissement assurent une bonne discipline et fixent des règles à respecter.

(a) The teachers are encouraging and show concern for their pupils.

(b) The school is well equipped with pleasant surroundings.

(c) It is a lively school with a lot going on.

(d) Discipline is good.

2   There is really only one negative point made by this pupil. What is it?

Cette élève n'évoque qu'un seul point négatif: qu'est-ce que c'est?

3   Find in the text the French equivalents of the following words and expressions.

Trouvez dans le texte l'équivalent français des mots et expressions suivants.

(a) They're interested in our problems.

(b) Computers.

(c) The atmosphere.

(d) Outings.

(e) Pleasant surroundings.

(f) It (the school) takes part in competitions.

(g) Rules to be observed.

Listen now to Anne-Catherine and Fabienne talking about the two advantages of Blanche de Castille as they see it: *les études* and *les amies*. The two girls speak fairly clearly, but they use some complex expressions you may not recognize at first.

Activité 15
15 MINUTES

AUDIO 8

1   Listen to the audio extract and try to understand the main points.

Écoutez l'extrait et essayez d'en comprendre l'essentiel.

Pour vous aider

avoir son bac   to pass the *baccalauréat* (examination marking the end of secondary school and allowing access to university studies)

des études supérieures   higher education

on vieillit   we get older

on mûrit   we become mature

on se fait des amies durables   we make lasting friendships

on arrive vraiment à créer des liens très forts   we really do manage to develop very strong ties

2   To check you have understood the gist of what the girls are saying, choose the most appropriate summaries from the alternatives given below.

Choisissez la phrase qui résume le mieux ce que disent les deux jeunes filles.

Les études

(a) Girls at Blanche de Castille have an advantage as far as their studies are concerned because the classes there are very small and the teaching is better than average.

(b) Many of the girls at Blanche de Castille don't want to go on to further study and the school offers them a wide variety of more vocationally oriented courses.

(c) At Blanche de Castille it is almost guaranteed that the girls will pass their *baccalauréat* and the school's reputation should help when it comes to going on to higher education.

Les amies

(d) The longer you stay at the school, the less you miss your friends outside.

(e) As you progress through the school, the more lasting friendships you make.

(f) Being with each other all the time means that friendships are often broken.

Expressing change with 'plus … plus' and 'moins … moins'

In commenting on life at Blanche de Castille, Fabienne said:

> **Plus** *on monte dans les classes,* **plus** *on vieillit,* **plus** *on mûrit,* **plus** *on se fait des amies durables.*
> The more you go up through the school, the older you get, the more mature you become, the more lasting friendships you make.

The same construction can be used with *moins*. For example:

> **Moins** *vous lisez,* **moins** *vous avez envie de lire.*
> The less you read, the less you want to read.

This construction is frequently used in sayings or to make generalizations. For example, one saying you may have heard is *plus ça change,* which in French is always followed by *plus c'est la même chose.*

You should note, however, that in written French if a *plus* or *moins* clause of this type contains *du, de la* or *des*, these become *de* (or *d'*). Fabienne was using relaxed spoken French when she said '*plus on se fait des amies durables*'. In writing the correct form would be: *plus on se fait d'amies durables.*

In the next *activité*, try your hand at writing some sentences in French using this construction. You can, of course, make sentences starting with *plus* followed by *moins,* and vice versa.

Activité 16
15 MINUTES

1 Match up the two halves of the lists below to make coherent sentences. There may be several possibilities!

Associez les moitiés de phrases pour construire des phrases cohérentes. Il y a parfois plusieurs possibilités!

(a) Plus on fixe de règles,

(b) Plus je lis d'œuvres philosophiques,

(c) Plus on fait de sport,

(d) Plus on sort,

(e) Moins je mange,

(f) Plus on regarde les informations à la télévision,

(i) plus on se détend.

(ii) plus on se fait d'amis.

(iii) moins les gens les respectent.

(iv) plus on se sent impuissant face aux problèmes du monde.

(v) moins je m'intéresse à la philosophie.

(vi) moins j'ai envie de manger.

2 Now invent some of your own 'sayings' by completing the sentences below with your own words.

Maintenant utilisez votre imagination pour compléter les phrases suivantes selon vos propres idées.

(a) Plus on vieillit,…

(b) Moins on travaille,…

(c) Plus on étudie la grammaire française,…

(d) Moins on parle,…

More about the use of 'en' + present participle

In the discussion you heard earlier in Audio Extract 8 the following two phrases were used:

> **En entrant** ici on est presque, pratiquement sûre d'avoir son bac.

> **En vivant** presque vingt-quatre heures sur vingt-quatre les unes avec les autres, on arrive vraiment… à créer des liens très forts.

Here, the construction *en* + present participle is not used to describe two things happening simultaneously, as was the case with Fabienne's description of the morning routine. Rather it explains how one event is brought about by another. The examples above could be translated literally as 'by coming here, you're almost certain to pass your *baccalauréat*' and 'by living with each other for twenty-four hours a day, we really do manage to develop very strong ties'. As you saw when you did *Activité 4* in Section 1, it's not always easy to find a translation of the *en* + present participle construction.

The *en* + present participle construction is useful when replying to certain questions beginning with *'comment?'*. For example:

> *Comment est-ce qu'on réussit aux examens?*
> How does one pass exams?
>
> *En travaillant dur!*
> By working hard!

Activité 17 invites you to put this into practice immediately – *en écoutant votre cassette!* First you need to check that you can pronounce the word for a manual, *un manuel* [man૫εl].

Activité 17
5   MINUTES

AUDIO   9

In this audio extract you'll hear a series of questions starting with *'comment?'*. Use the construction *en* + present participle in your replies. You'll hear prompts in English which will tell you what to say.

Écoutez les questions et répondez selon les suggestions qui sont données en anglais.

1.3 Pension prison

By now you have probably formed some picture of life in a French boarding school, but it may be useful at this stage to fit this information into a wider context and find out briefly how the school system is organized in France and what is the status of private schools such as Blanche de Castille. This information, presented in the short text below, should also help you understand some of the references in an interview with Anne-Catherine, where she explains how she came to be sent away to boarding school.

Activité 18
20   MINUTES

1   *Lisez le texte qui suit.*

L'enseignement secondaire en France

L'organisation de l'enseignement secondaire

L'école en France est obligatoire à partir de six ans et jusqu'à seize ans. La plupart des enfants quittent l'école primaire à l'âge de onze ans pour entrer au collège.

L'année d'entrée au collège s'appelle la sixième. Ensuite les élèves passent en cinquième et ainsi de suite jusqu'à la troisième. Pendant la sixième et la cinquième, tous les élèves suivent le même programme. À partir de la quatrième, il y a la possibilité de choisir certaines options et à la fin de la troisième tous les élèves passent un examen national, le brevet des collèges. C'est après le brevet que les élèves peuvent choisir de quitter le collège ou de continuer leurs études au lycée. Il faut passer trois années au lycée (la seconde, la première et la terminale) pour préparer le baccalauréat. À la fin de l'année, un élève qui a des difficultés scolaires peut 'redoubler', c'est-à-dire rester dans la même classe deux années de suite, si ses parents le demandent et si ses professeurs sont d'accord. Souvent, les professeurs préfèrent changer l'orientation de l'élève. Il existe aussi des lycées professionnels où l'on peut préparer en deux ans un diplôme professionnel. La plupart des lycéens passent le baccalauréat à l'âge de dix-huit ans. Ceux qui réussissent ont le droit de s'inscrire dans une université pour poursuivre des études supérieures.

L'enseignement privé

L'enseignement public en France est résolument 'laïc', c'est-à-dire neutre en matière de religion et de politique. 83% des élèves poursuivent leurs études secondaires dans des collèges et lycées publics. Par contre, la plupart des établissements privés sont catholiques, mais ce n'est pas toujours pour des raisons religieuses que les parents mettent leurs enfants dans des écoles privées. Ces établissements ont souvent la réputation d'être plus attentifs à la discipline et aux besoins individuels de chaque élève. Il existe aussi des établissements privés appelés 'boîtes à bac' qui permettent aux jeunes qui ont échoué au lycée d'obtenir quand même leur bac!

Pour vous aider

et ainsi de suite   and so on and so forth

changer l'orientation de l'élève   to change the subjects taken by the pupil

lycées professionnels   colleges (offering vocational courses at secondary level)

diplôme professionnel   vocational qualification

neutre   neutral

en matière de   as regards

qui permettent aux jeunes... d'obtenir   which enable young people... to obtain

2   *Complétez les phrases suivantes.*

(a) In France children start school at the age of_____ and can leave when they are _____ .

(b) The sixth form in Great Britain corresponds to_____
and _____ in the French school system.

(c) A pupil who is *en quatrième* is likely to be _____
years old.

(d) In the French system pupils who have grave difficulty coping with the
syllabus may have to _____ .

(e) The preparation for the *baccalauréat* normally lasts_____years.

(f) A *boîte à bac* is a French private school which has a reputation for

_____ .

Before listening to the interview with Anne-Catherine we want you to do
some pronunciation work on sounds which occur a lot in the imperfect and
the perfect tenses. It's not always easy to hear the difference between the two
since their pronunciation can be fairly similar, for example, *je mangeais*
[ʒəmɑ̃ʒɛ] and *j'ai mangé* [ʒemɑ̃ʒe]. When you're speaking, try to make sure
you distinguish the two tenses by making (and even exaggerating) the
difference between *je* and *j'ai*.

Activité 19
1 5 M I N U T E S

A U D I O   1 0

1 The pairs of words below illustrate the difference between the sounds [ə]
and [ɛ]. Listen to how these words are pronounced on the first part of
Audio Extract 10.

Écoutez ces paires de mots qui démontrent la différence entre les sons [ə]
et [ɛ].

le	les
des	de
mes	me
ce	ces
te	tes
j'ai	je

2 Now listen to the second part of the audio extract and repeat the
following sentences in the gaps that have been left. Pay particular
attention to the sounds [ə] and [ɛ].

*Maintenant, écoutez la deuxième partie de l'extrait et répétez ces phrases
qui démontrent la différence entre les sons* [ə] *et* [ɛ].

• Je mangeais, j'ai mangé.

• Avant, je mangeais beaucoup de bonbons.

- Hier, j'ai mangé à la crêperie.

- Je parlais, j'ai parlé.

- Autrefois, je parlais bien espagnol.

- Hier soir, j'ai parlé à ma sœur au téléphone.

- Je marchais, j'ai marché.

- Il y a dix ans, je marchais cinq kilomètres tous les jours.

- Hier, j'ai marché cinq cents mètres et j'étais épuisée.

So why was Anne-Catherine sent to Blanche de Castille? Apparently she was *'une fille assez désolante pour mes parents'* (a great disappointment to my parents). She went to Blanche de Castille so that she could, as she puts it, *'me remettre un peu dans le droit chemin'* (get myself back on the straight and narrow). Listen now to her story. *Activité 20* is designed to help you understand what she says and in *Activité 21* you'll focus on a grammatical point: Anne-Catherine's use of past tenses.

Activité 20
20 MINUTES

AUDIO 11

1   Anne-Catherine tells her story clearly and in a lively manner, but she does use some idiomatic expressions which you may not immediately catch. To help you, we have listed six of the key ones below with a set of English translations. Listen to the audio extract once, paying particular attention to the French expressions listed on the left. Match each one with its English translation in the right-hand list.

Écoutez l'extrait pour repérer les phrases qui se trouvent à gauche. Ensuite, regardez à droite et choisissez la traduction anglaise de chacune.

(a) Je voyais des gens pas très fréquentables.	(i) I'm not a very well brought up young lady.
(b) On me menaçait de me mettre en pension.	(ii) I thought everything was going to collapse around me.
(c) J'ai fait une très mauvaise seconde.	(iii) I used to mix with bad company.
(d) J'ai cru que tout allait s'écrouler autour de moi.	(iv) I did really badly in my fifth year.
(e) Je suis arrivée ici en pleurant.	(v) They threatened to send me to boarding school.
(f) Je ne suis pas une fille comme il faut.	(vi) I arrived here in tears.

2   Now you have identified the meaning of the key expressions, listen to the audio extract again and indicate whether the following statements are true

or false. In the case of false statements, note down the correct answer in French.

Réécoutez l'extrait et indiquez si les phrases suivantes sont vraies ou fausses. Dans le cas d'une phrase fausse, notez la réponse correcte en français.

	Vrai	Faux
(a) Avant d'aller à Blanche de Castille, Anne-Catherine travaillait dur à l'école.	❏	❏
(b) Pour Anne-Catherine, Blanche de Castille était une école très stricte, très bourgeoise.	❏	❏
(c) Anne-Catherine est allée à Blanche de Castille après sa sixième.	❏	❏
(d) Anne-Catherine était contente d'aller à Blanche de Castille.	❏	❏

We're now going to look at Anne-Catherine's story from the point of view of the two tenses she uses in her narrative: the imperfect and the perfect. Before doing the next *activité*, you might like to remind yourself of the formation of these two tenses and the contexts in which each one is used (see *Cadences*, Book 1, Section 2).

You may have already noticed in Audio Extract 11 that Anne-Catherine says *'Je suis arrivée'*, using *être* and not *avoir* to form the perfect tense. Although *avoir* occurs with more verbs, certain verbs form their perfect tense with *être*. You will be returning to this point in Book 4 of *Cadences*, but if you want more information on this now, look at page 106 in your Grammar Book.

Activité 21
20 MINUTES

AUDIO 11

1 In explaining why she was sent to Blanche de Castille, Anne-Catherine starts by giving some background information about what she used to be like. Listen to Audio Extract 11 again and underline the correct form of the verb in the transcript below.

Réécoutez l'extrait et soulignez la forme du verbe qui convient.

Avant, j'étais/j'ai été une fille assez, euh, désolante pour mes parents, selon mes parents. C'est-à-dire que je suis sortie/je sortais beaucoup, je voyais/j'ai vu des gens pas très fréquentables et, euh, je tournais mal/j'ai mal tourné, et je travaillais pas/j'ai pas travaillé à l'école. Depuis la sixième, c'est-à-dire vers dix ans, on m'a menacée/on me menaçait de me mettre en pension à Blanche de Castille, c'est-à-dire une école très stricte; et pour moi, Blanche de Castille c'était/ça a été vraiment, euh, les bourgeois, le..., le style vraiment particulier d'aristocrates.

2   The second part of Anne Catherine's story is somewhat different. Rather than describing the background, she recounts the sequence of events leading up to being sent to Blanche de Castille. Again, listen to the audio extract and underline the correct form of the verb in the transcript below.

Réécoutez l'extrait et soulignez la forme du verbe qui convient.

Donc j'ai…, j'ai fait/je faisais une très mauvaise seconde, et on m'a autorisée/on m'autorisait à redoubler; et, euh, donc on m'a dit/on me disait: 'Anne-Catherine, tu vas aller en pension à Blanche de Castille.' Alors là, j'ai cru/je croyais que tout allait s'écrouler autour de moi, c'était/ça a été vraiment l'enfer… Et donc je suis arrivée/j'arrivais ici en pleurant, 'Je vous en prie, ne m'acceptez pas, je suis pas une fille comme il faut'; et finalement, ben, ils m'ont acceptée/ils m'acceptaient pour justement resserrer la vis.

Distinguishing between the imperfect and the perfect tenses

In Book 1 of *Cadences* you learned how to use the imperfect tense to talk about past habits (what you used to do) and you probably already know a little about how to use the perfect tense. It is important to extend your ability to choose between these tenses as they are both very widely used in writing and in conversation.

In the first part of Audio Extract 11 the verbs are in the imperfect tense. They are used to describe past habits and can be translated by the English 'used to':

Je sortais beaucoup.
I used to go out a lot.

The imperfect can also be used to describe a state of affairs in the past that lasted for some time:

J'étais une fille assez désolante pour mes parents.
I was a great disappointment to my parents.

It is used, too, in order to talk about things that were still happening, in other words, about events which were continuing at the moment being talked about.

On me menaçait de me mettre en pension.
They were threatening to send me to boarding school.

The second part of Audio Extract 11 is mainly in the perfect tense because it narrates completed events or actions.

Je suis arrivée ici en pleurant.
I arrived here in tears.

The distinction between the perfect and imperfect tenses is not one that can be grasped quickly. As you read and listen to more French, you will come across examples where the choice between the two is not clear-cut but reflects a particular shade of meaning. It will take you some time to acquire a sensitivity to this. For thc moment, all we want you to do is to make a start at building up your knowledge of this area by applying the categories outlined above. The following *activité* encourages you to think about why one tense is chosen rather than another.

Activité 22
1 5   M I N U T E S

In the following text an ex-pupil from another institution, Notre Dame des Fleurs, recounts her memories of the school. Read the text and then look in particular at the verbs. For each verb in the past, make a brief note about why the perfect or imperfect tense was used.

Dans le texte suivant justifiez l'emploi du passé composé et de l'imparfait.

Je suis entrée à Notre Dame des Fleurs en 1985. À cette époque-là, l'école était beaucoup plus petite que maintenant. Il n'y avait que vingt-cinq jeunes filles. On portait un uniforme que tout le monde détestait. On se levait à six heures et demie tous les matins. L'enfer! Il y avait beaucoup de contraintes. La discipline était très stricte. On n'avait pas le droit de parler pendant les repas.

Mais c'était une école très bien équipée. Il y avait un laboratoire de langues et beaucoup d'ordinateurs. En 1987 j'ai passé mon baccalauréat mais la première fois je ne l'ai pas réussi. J'ai redoublé et l'année suivante j'ai eu mon bac. J'ai quitté Notre Dame des Fleurs en 1988 et, par la suite, j'ai fait un diplôme d'informatique que j'ai terminé en 1992. Je travaille maintenant pour une société qui fabrique des ordinateurs.

Pour vous aider

diplôme d'informatique   computing qualification

Faites le bilan

When you have finished this section of the book, you should be able to:

- Use the following phrases to state what you must do: *il faut, on est obligé(e) de* and *on doit* (*Activités 2, 3, 9* and *10*).

- Use the following phrases to state what is not allowed: *il est interdit de, n'avoir pas le droit de* + infinitive, *ne pas pouvoir* and *être interdit* (*Activités 6, 7, 9* and *10*).

- Understand and use the structures *plus … plus* and *moins … moins* (*Activité 16*).

- Use the structure *en* + present participle in answer to the question *'comment?'* (*Activité 17*).

- Pronounce the sounds [ə] and [ɛ] intelligibly (*Activité 19*).

- Understand the distinction between the perfect and imperfect tenses (*Activité 22*).

Vocabulaire à retenir

1.1 Une journée à Blanche de Castille

un cours

un pensionnaire, une pensionnaire

un règlement

empêcher quelqu'un de travailler

être le bienvenu/la bienvenue

être au courant de

n'oublie pas tes affaires

faire sa toilette

1.2 Contraintes et avantages

une contrainte

faire du bruit

laisser la lumière allumée

s'intéresser à

un ordinateur

une ambiance

une sortie

un cadre agréable

participer à un concours

fixer des règles

respecter des règles

se faire des ami(e)s

créer des liens

le bac(calauréat)

avoir son bac(calauréat)

les études supérieures

1.3 Pension prison

suivre des cours

redoubler

choisir une option

permettre à quelqu'un de faire quelque chose

avoir des difficultés scolaires

s'inscrire dans une université

mettre un(e) élève en pension

2 À l'armée

STUDY CHART

	Topic	Activity/timing	Audio/video	Key points
1 br 20 mins	2.1 Le service national	23 (15 mins)		Vocabulary: military service
		24 (30 mins)		
		25 (10 mins)	Audio	Pronouncing the sound [sj]
		26 (10 mins)		Vocabulary building: recognizing patterns in word formation
2 brs 50 mins	2.2 La vie de caserne	27 (30 mins)	Video	Understanding the video sequence: military service
		28 (15 mins)	Video	
		29 (15 mins)	Video	
		30 (5 mins)		Using *même* in comparisons
		31 (10 mins)	Audio	Using *même* orally
		32 (15 mins)		Using *arriver à*
		33 (15 mins)		Writing about your needs using *avoir besoin de*
		34 (25 mins)		Describing a conscript's routine in writing
		35 (15 mins)	Video	Recognizing expressions of dislike
2 brs 10 mins	2.3 Le bon parcours	36 (35 mins)	Video	Understanding expressions for likes, dislikes and enthusiasms
		37 (15 mins)	Video	
		38 (15 mins)	Audio	Expressing likes and dislikes
		39 (15 mins)		Using perfect and imperfect tenses
		40 (45 mins)		Section revision

Replaced by Appel de préparation à la défense

29

*I*n this section you will be finding out about national service (*service national*) in France, an event which figures large in the lives of most young men. To give you some background information on national service and its various forms, we begin with a couple of short informative texts. You can then get an idea of what military life looks and feels like by watching video sequences in which four young conscripts (*appelés* or *conscrits*) from barracks in Angers give their views on the positive and negative aspects of military service.

As you work through this section, you'll come across more ways to express likes and dislikes and you'll build on the structures you studied in Section 1 for talking about restrictions and obligation.

En rang pour aller déjeuner

2.1 Le service national

The first text, *Le service national,* presents the key facts and figures about national service in France. As you will see, there are basically two types: *la forme militaire,* which involves service in a military unit, and *les formes civiles,* the various non-military options. The second text, *Un service national sous une forme civile,* provides you with more detailed information on the non-military options.

Activité 23
15 MINUTES

Read the text *Le service national* and the associated statistics and then tick the correct answers to the following statements.

Lisez le texte et les chiffres qui vont avec. Ensuite, cochez la réponse qui complète correctement les phrases qui suivent.

1 Le service national en France dure:

   (a) dix mois ❑

   (b) deux ans ❑

2 Le service national existe depuis:

    (a) la fin de la deuxième guerre mondiale   ❑

    (b) la Révolution française   ❑

3 La grande majorité des appelés font leur service dans:

    (a) l'armée de l'air   ❑

    (b) l'armée de terre   ❑

4 La majorité des appelés font un service:

    (a) militaire   ❑

    (b) civil   ❑

5 Parmi les jeunes, il y a:

    (a) 1,74% d'objecteurs de conscience   ❑

    (b) 0,18% d'objecteurs de conscience   ❑

Le Service national

La France a choisi pour sa défense de faire appel à la contribution de chaque citoyen

Elle demande à chaque jeune garçon Français de participer pendant un an de sa vie à cette défense.

Il s'agit d'un choix ancien remontant à la Révolution française qui a été maintenu par tous les régimes depuis 200 ans.

265 000 jeunes y sont appelés chaque année.

Le Service national s'organise autour d'une forme militaire et de formes civiles.

FORME MILITAIRE

10 mois
94% des appelés répartis entre:

67,3% l'armée de terre
8,1% la marine nationale
14% l'armée de l'air
3,5% la gendarmerie
1,1% autres

FORMES CIVILES

6% des appelés répartis entre:

1,8% le service de la coopération: 16 mois
0,3% l'aide technique: 16 mois
1,98% la police nationale: 10 mois
1,74% les objecteurs de conscience: 20 mois
0,18% la sécurité civile: 10 mois

Chiffres datant de 1992.

(*Quid 1991*, p. 15)

Les formes civiles

As the previous text indicates, non-military national service in France can take a number of forms. There is *le service de la coopération*, which involves work abroad, and *l'aide technique*, where those with professional training can serve in France's overseas territories, known as the DOM-TOM. Conscripts can also work for *la police nationale* or, in the case of *objecteurs de conscience,* undertake a form of community service.

en passant » » » »

The inhabitants of the Caribbean islands of Martinique and Guadeloupe (*la Martinique et la Guadeloupe*) are entitled to vote in French general elections and to send representatives to the national parliament in Paris. They are French citizens, just like those of Paris or Marseilles. Martinique and Guadeloupe are both *départements d'outre-mer*, or DOM, and they are administered exactly like any *département* in metropolitan France. The other DOM are the island of Reunion (*la Réunion*) in the Indian Ocean and French Guiana (*la Guyane*) in South America.

The TOM are *territoires d'outre-mer*, remnants of France's colonial empire, and these are scattered across the Pacific, from New Caledonia (*la Nouvelle-Calédonie*) to French Polynesia. The TOM are not an integral part of France like the DOM, but the links remain very close.

Many other countries that were formerly part of the colonial empire have also retained close economic and cultural ties with France and many of them have signed co-operation agreements (*des accords de coopération*) with France, for example Mali and Senegal (*le Mali et le Sénégal*).

» » » »

To find out more about the different forms of non-military national service, we want you to read another short text. You will probably find this text more complex than the previous one. Rather than trying to understand every word, take a more selective approach, aiming simply to glean enough information to complete the next *activité*.

Activité 24
30 MINUTES

1 Read the text *Un service national sous une forme civile*, then indicate on the table on page 34 which details apply to which of the non-military options listed. You can do this by putting the letter representing each option – (a), (b), (c), etc. – against the relevant details. This has already been done for (a) *le service de la coopération*. You will find that some of the details apply to several forms of service.

Lisez le texte et identifiez dans le tableau de la page 34 les détails qui s'appliquent à chaque forme civile.

UN SERVICE NATIONAL SOUS UNE FORME CIVILE

Il existe des formes civiles du Service national, destinées à répondre aux autres besoins de la Défense, ainsi qu'aux impératifs de solidarité. Ces formes civiles de Service national concernent 6 % des appelés (16 600 postes en 1992).

*S*ERVICE DE LA COOPERATION :
5 000 postes en 92.
Durée du service : seize mois

Je possède un diplôme d'enseignement supérieur et souhaite participer au développement des pays avec lesquels la France a signé un accord de coopération.
Je peux effectuer un service au titre de la COOPERATION technique (ingénieurs, chercheurs, médecins), culturelle (enseignants), ou en entreprise. Je possède un diplôme professionnel (CAP, BEP), je peux participer au projet GLOBUS (action humanitaire).

*A*IDE TECHNIQUE
850 postes en 92.
Durée du service : seize mois.

Je souhaite partir outre-mer et possède le niveau de technicien supérieur.

Je peux effectuer un service actif au titre de l'AIDE TECHNIQUE dans les départements et territoires d'outre-mer dans les activités suivantes :
• Enseignement, action sanitaire et sociale, travaux publics, développement rural, recherche, informatique, transports.

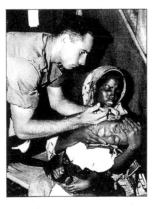

*O*BJECTEUR DE CONSCIENCE
4 950 appelés en 92.
Durée du service : vingt mois.

Si pour des motifs de conscience, je suis personnellement opposé à l'usage des armes : je peux demander avant le 15 du mois qui précède mon incorporation, à effectuer le service civil des objecteurs de conscience et serai mis à la disposition du ministère chargé des Affaires sociales.

*P*OLICE NATIONALE
5 600 postes en 92.
Durée du service : dix mois.

Si je veux aider la police nationale dans ses tâches de prévention et d'assistance.
Je peux faire acte de candidature à cette forme de service. On me confiera des emplois touchant :
• à la circulation,
• à l'accueil du public,
• au contrôle.
Je peux être volontaire pour un service long.

*S*ECURITE CIVILE
500 postes environ en 93.
Durée du service : dix mois

Cette forme de service prévue par la loi du 4 janvier 1992 s'effectue soit à la Direction ou dans les Etats Majors de zones de la sécurité civile, soit au sein d'un service départemental d'incendie et de secours.

(*Service national, vous et nous, un service à se rendre.* Dossier d'information no. 98, septembre 1993)

Pour vous aider

je souhaite I would like

outre-mer overseas

le niveau the level (here: academic level)

effectuer to carry out

serai mis à la disposition du will be placed at the disposal of

faire acte de candidature apply

on me confiera I will be given

l'accueil du public dealing with the public

Non-military option	Activities include	Place of work	Length of service
(a) Service de la coopération	Traffic control *c*	France *a*	16 months (a) *b*
	Computing *b*	Other foreign countries (a)	20 months *d*
(b) Aide technique	Engineering (a) *b*		10 months *c*
(c) Police nationale	Research (a) *b*	DOM-TOM *b*	
(d) Objecteur de conscience	Social work *b* *d*		
	Teaching (a) *b*		

2　Skim through the text again, this time to identify the French expressions which correspond to the English words below.

Trouvez dans le texte l'équivalent français des mots ci-dessous.

(a) researchers　(b) teachers　(c) engineers

3　Read the following descriptions of young men who are thinking of opting for a non-military form of national service. From your understanding of the text and the notes you made in step 1 above, suggest which *forme civile* each young man might apply for. Note the length of time the appropriate form of national service would last.

Lisez ci-dessous les profils de quatre jeunes gens qui pensent choisir une forme civile du service national. Proposez la forme civile qui à votre avis convient le mieux à chaque jeune homme et notez la durée du service qu'il doit effectuer.

(a) **Hervé Desforges** a fait des études de médecine. Il connaît bien le Maroc et aimerait bien faire son service national là-bas.

Forme civile:　　　　　　　　　　　Durée:

(b) **Jean-Paul Peraud** est instituteur. Dans le cadre de ses études, il a fait de la psychologie sociale. Il adore voyager.

Forme civile:　　　　　　　　　　　Durée:

(c) **Alain Latour** est bénévole dans une association qui aide les jeunes qui sortent de prison. Il est pacifiste et veut faire son service national en France.

Forme civile:　　　　　　　　　　　Durée:

(d) **Simon Leclerc** a une formation d'ingénieur en informatique et rêve de partir à l'île de la Réunion, car son amie est réunionnaise.

Forme civile:　　　　　　　　　　　Durée:

The text that you have just read contains the following words that English speakers sometimes pronounce incorrectly:

> coopéra**ti**on, na**ti**onale, con**sci**ence, techni**ci**en, préven**ti**on, circula**ti**on

Whereas in English the sound of the letters in bold type is [ʃ], in French it is [sj]. In English, emphasis is placed on the syllables shown next in bold – pre**ven**tion, **con**science. In French, for all the words above except *nationale*, the stress falls at the end of the word – préven**tion**, con**science**.

The next *activité* gives you the chance to practise recognizing and producing these sounds. It also gives you similar practice with the [R] sound. Check on your Phonetics Cassette first if you feel you need to.

Activité 25
10 MINUTES
AUDIO 12

1 In the first part of this audio extract you will hear a number of phrases. Listen carefully to their pronunciation and then repeat them, paying particular attention to the [sj] sound. Remember to emphasize the final syllable of the words containing this sound, where appropriate.

Écoutez et répétez les mots que vous entendez. Faites bien attention au son [sj] au milieu des mots et mettez bien l'accent sur la syllabe finale lorsque c'est nécessaire.

2 The second part of the audio extract gives you the chance to practise the [R] sound in different places in words – at the beginning of a word, between two vowels in the middle of a word, at the end of a word, and either before or after a consonant. Listen carefully to the examples and then repeat them as often as you need to.

Écoutez et répétez les mots que vous entendez. Essayez de bien prononcer le son [R].

Building up vocabulary

Recognizing families of words and seeing how nouns, verbs, adjectives and adverbs relate to each other is an important skill to develop. In Book 1 of *Cadences* we suggested that one useful way of extending your vocabulary is to collect families of words and to learn related nouns and verbs together. The dictionary gives you a way to do this, providing you read it 'vertically'. Suppose you want to acquire some vocabulary based around the idea of 'organizing' and 'organization'. Look up *organis-* in the French side of your dictionary and let your eye wander up and down the alphabetical list of headwords: you'll probably find five words or so containing *organis-* in the list. You might want to note all of them down, but the verb and some of the nouns are the most useful ones to collect. The verb ends in *-er* and the noun with the longest entry ends in *-ation*.

You could use your dossier to record related nouns and verbs according to their endings, as follows:

-er	*-ation*
organis-er	une organis-ation
détermin-er	la détermin-ation
présent-er	une présent-ation
limit-er	une limit-ation

In addition to teaching yourself some vocabulary, you will also have learned a pattern of word formation that will enable you to guess how a noun is written on the basis of knowing a related verb, or vice-versa. You will then be able to predict the shape of many words: *conservation* from *conserver*, *élaboration* from *élaborer*, and so on.

This is one of the commonest patterns of word formation in French. There are others, however, which you might also like to record. For instance:

-er	*-e*
limit-er	une limit-e
contrast-er	un contrast-e

-er	*-ion*
précis-er	une précis-ion
object-er	une object-ion

-er	*-ement*
enregistr-er	un enregistr-ement
renvers-er	un renvers-ement

-dre	*-te*
déten-dre	la déten-te
atten-dre	une atten-te

The next *activité* is designed to help you recognize patterns in word formation. There will be further practice of this in Section 3.

Activité 26
1 0   M I N U T E S

Complete the table opposite with the correct forms of the verbs and nouns. Have a guess at what they are first and then re-read the text *Un service national sous une forme civile* (page 33) to see if your guesses were right.

Remplissez les cases vides du tableau ci-contre. Pour chaque mot donné, trouvez dans le texte 'Un service national sous une forme civile' le verbe ou le nom qui correspond.

Verbe	*Nom*
participer	la participation
circuler	
enseigner	
servir	
	la demande
durer	
coopérer	
développer	
assister	
chercher	
accueillir	

2.2 La vie de caserne

You now have some background understanding of *le service national* and, in particular, of the different possibilities for young men who choose one of the *formes civiles*. The video that you're going to watch next concentrates on *la forme militaire* and is based on interviews with four *appelés*, Éric, Stéphane, Christophe and Olivier, who are nearing the end of their military service in an engineers regiment, the 21ème (vingt-et-unième) Régiment du Génie, at Angers.

The video is made up of three sequences: *La vie de caserne,* where we see the conscripts on and off duty; *Qu'est-ce que vous n'aimez pas ici?*, where the conscripts explain what they find unpleasant or annoying about military service, and *Le bon parcours,* which shows them undertaking one of the most physically demanding aspects of their training, the assault course (*le parcours d'obstacles*).

The first sequence starts with a general introduction in which you see the conscripts involved in various military exercises. They then comment on the camaraderie which develops between them during their ten months together in the barracks (*la caserne*), but also on their need for privacy from time to time.

Manœuvres sur le pont mobile

1   Read through the list below, then watch the first video sequence (42:33–46:50). As you watch, tick off the things you see from the list. Three of the items in the list are not on the video. Which are they?

Avant de regarder la première séquence vidéo, lisez attentivement la liste ci-dessous. En regardant la vidéo, cochez les choses que vous voyez. Quelles sont les trois choses qui n'apparaissent pas à l'image?

(a) Les conscrits à l'exercice.   ❏

(b) Un avion qui décolle d'un aéroport militaire.   ❏

(c) Une voiture qui entre dans la caserne.   ❏

(d) Des conscrits en train de manœuvrer un pont mobile.   ❏

(e) Un conscrit qui conduit un véhicule-école.   ❏

(f) Le bureau du commandant.   ❏

(g) Une chambre de caserne.   ❏

(h) Des conscrits qui jouent au billard.   ❏

(i) Des conscrits en train de ranger leurs affaires.   ❏

(j) Des conscrits en train de faire leur toilette.   ❏

(k) Des conscrits qui lisent.   ❏

2 Read through the following statements and identify which are true and which are false. Correct the false ones in French if you can. Then watch this video sequence again to check your answers.

Lisez les assertions suivantes et indiquez si elles sont vraies ou fausses. Corrigez en français les assertions qui sont fausses. Regardez la séquence une deuxième fois pour vérifier vos réponses.

	Vrai	Faux
(a) En général, le service national se fait à l'âge de vingt ans.	❑	❑
(b) La grande majorité passe dix mois à la caserne.	❑	❑
(c) Les conscrits du 21ème Régiment du Génie sont formés comme techniciens.	❑	❑
(d) Ils ont l'occasion pendant leur service d'obtenir le permis de conduire.	❑	❑
(e) En général, les conscrits interviewés apprécient la vie en collectivité.	❑	❑
(f) Ils ont beaucoup de moments seuls pendant la journée.	❑	❑

Pour vous aider

enrichissante enriching

rendre service be helpful

milieux sociaux social backgrounds

une certaine amitié a kind of friendship

pas forcément not necessarily

le même niveau d'études the same standard of education

les mêmes goûts the same tastes

(bien) s'entendre to get on (well) together

c'est pas toujours évident it's not always easy (note the dropped *ne* characteristic of spoken French)

Now that you have understood the gist of this first sequence, the next *activité* takes you back to work more intensively on the interviews with the four conscripts – Éric, Stéphane, Christophe and Olivier.

Activité 28
15 MINUTES
V I D E O

Overleaf are some of the comments made by the four conscripts we interviewed, but they are not presented in the order that you heard them on the video. Watch the video sequence again (44:15–46:50) and identify who says what.

Visionnez de nouveau la séquence vidéo où les quatre appelés parlent de leur vie à la caserne. Pour chacune des phrases suivantes, identifiez la personne qui parle.

Eric   1   À l'école, j'avais vécu un peu à l'internat, donc je sais ce que c'est de vivre avec plusieurs dans une chambre.

Stephan   2   Au service national, j'aime beaucoup la vie en communauté.

————   3   Chacun doit faire un petit effort, parfois un gros effort.

Olivi...   4   La vie privée? Ah, elle est assez difficile à, en fait à préserver durant la journée.

Eric   5   On s'amuse, on plaisante, on passe de bons moments.

To check your understanding of what the conscripts say, answer the questions below. You will need to watch the second part of the sequence again (45:32–46:50) as this *activité* requires you to note down particular expressions that the young men use.

Activité 29
15 MINUTES

V I D E O

1   For Stéphane, contact with people from all walks of life (*des gens de milieux sociaux différents*) is one of the positive aspects of military service. Christophe also mentions that he likes the chance to meet different people. But different in what way? Watch the video (45:32–46.50) and fill in his missing words below, using the verbs in the box.

Complétez le texte avec les mots de l'encadré.

Il y a la vie en collectivité, le fait que l'on se retrouve avec des gens que l'on ne connaissait pas du tout, qui sont pas forcément du même ___âge___ que moi, qui n'ont pas forcément, je dirais les mêmes, le même niveau d' ___études___ , les mêmes ___goûts___ .

> études, âge, goûts

2   At the end of this sequence, Christophe tells us that he sometimes feels the need to be alone – *j'ai besoin d'être seul*. But for what reasons? Fill in his missing words, choosing from the selection in the box below.

Complétez le texte avec les mots de l'encadré.

J'ai souvent besoin de petits moments où j'ai besoin d'être seul, que ce soit pour ___lire___ , pour ___penser___ , pour ___écrire___ , enfin toutes ces choses-là, ou tout simplement pour ___être___ tranquille, sans bruit, et c'est vrai que là, c'est pas toujours évident quand vous êtes dans une chambre où il y cinq ou dix personnes.

> être, écrire, lire, penser

Using 'même' in comparisons

Christophe talks about people different in age from himself (*pas du même âge que moi*) and with different tastes (*pas les mêmes goûts*). Just like other adjectives, *même* agrees with the noun it describes, so an 's' is added when it refers to a plural noun such as *goûts* (see Grammar Book, pages 35 and 60).

In *Activités 30* and *31* you'll practise using *même* as an adjective, working with some of the expressions from the video sequence you've just watched.

Activité 30
5 MINUTES

Traduisez en français.

1 Éric is in the same regiment as Christophe.

2 Stéphane has not got the same tastes as Éric.

3 Christophe does not come from the same social background as Éric and Stéphane.

Activité 31
10 MINUTES

AUDIO 13

Listen to the audio extract. You are telling a French-speaking visitor about an evening class on local history that you are attending. After each English prompt, speak your answer out loud in French in the gap that has been left or record yourself. You will need to use some of the expressions you have heard on the video.

Écoutez l'extrait. Répondez en français aux questions, selon les suggestions données en anglais.

Using 'arriver à'

On the video Christophe talks very positively about the fact that, in general, the conscripts manage to get on fairly well, despite living so closely together. He refers to:

> le fait de vivre ensemble et finalement d'**arriver** en général **à** bien s'entendre.

Arriver à is the French expression which translates 'to manage to' and is followed by an infinitive. For example:

> *Es-tu arrivé à téléphoner au restaurant pour la réservation de ce soir?* Did you manage to phone the restaurant about the reservation for tonight?

In *Activité 32* you'll practise this very common and useful construction.

Activité 32
15 MINUTES

Imagine you are writing to a French friend about the problems of studying on your own. Translate the sentences below using *arriver à* and then write some more sentences of your own, describing things you can or can't manage to do.

Vous racontez à un(e) ami(e) les difficultés qu'on peut avoir quand on étudie une langue seul(e). Traduisez les phrases suivantes. Ensuite, inventez vos propres phrases pour dire ce que vous arrivez ou n'arrivez pas à faire.

1   I usually manage to understand the video.

2   I don't manage to find enough time to learn the vocabulary.

3   I can't manage to pronounce the 'r'.

4   _____

    _____

5   _____

    _____

Expressing needs using 'j'ai besoin de'

In the video sequence you've just watched, one of the conscripts commented on his need for time on his own:

> *J'ai besoin d'être seul.*
> I need to be on my own.

You can use the expression *j'ai besoin de* (with the 's' pronounced as [z]) to talk about a thing that you need:

> *J'ai besoin d'argent.*
> I need money.

You can also use it to talk about something you need to do:

> *J'ai besoin d'acheter du pain.*
> I need to buy some bread.

This means that the expression can be followed by either a noun or a verb in the infinitive. Practise this in the next *activité*.

Activité 33
15 MINUTES

1   Make four meaningful sentences by choosing one element from each column in the table opposite.

Faites quatre phrases en associant des éléments de chaque colonne dans le tableau ci-contre.

J'ai besoin de	argent	parce que je n'arrive pas à trouver les timbres que j'ai achetés hier.
Je n'ai pas besoin de	regarder les informations à la télévision	parce que Philippe va payer pour moi.
J'ai besoin d'	aller à la poste	parce que l'ordinateur corrige automatiquement l'orthographe.
Je n'ai pas besoin d'	dictionnaire	parce que je ne suis pas au courant du résultat des élections.

2   Now think of your own life and your own needs and complete the following sentences using *j'ai besoin de*.

Maintenant, complétez les phrases suivantes en employant l'expression 'j'ai besoin de'.

(a) Le week-end…

(b) En vacances…

(c) Au cours de la journée…

(d) Quand je suis stressé(e)…

(e) Quand j'ai des problèmes…

Now that you have worked fairly intensively on some of the phrases used in the interviews with the *appelés*, you might like to watch the video sequence (44:15–46:50) again before doing the next *activité*.

Activité 34
25 MINUTES

Imagine you're one of the soldiers in the dormitory you saw on the video. You're writing a short letter home, describing the scene around you and telling your family about your first few days in the barracks. Write a paragraph (about 60 to 100 words) in which you describe the people who share the room with you. Say how many there are, give them names and ages perhaps, say what they are doing now and what you did earlier in the day (in which case, you'll need to switch to using the perfect, and possibly the imperfect, tense). Try to reuse some of the vocabulary you've come across so far in this book. You could also use some of the verbs in the box on the next page. They are in the infinitive: remember that you need to alter the verb when you use it with the *je, nous* or *on* forms.

Écrivez une lettre à votre famille pour raconter vos premières expériences à l'armée. Utilisez les expressions de l'encadré de la page suivante, ou d'autres de votre choix.

> partager une chambre, jouer au billard, avoir le même âge, se reposer, plaisanter, discuter avec, passer de bons moments, ranger la chambre, faire l'exercice

Qu'est-ce que vous n'aimez pas ici?

In the next video sequence Stéphane, Christophe and Olivier reveal what they don't like about military life and, in answer to the interviewer's question *'Quelle est la règle la plus contraignante?'*, they comment on the rules which they find most restrictive. This introduces some more ways of expressing dislike.

Activité 35
1 5   M I N U T E S
V I D E O

1   Before watching the video, think of any French expressions you know that correspond to the English ones listed below. Then watch the video sequence (46:52–48:00) and tick the things the three conscripts dislike about military service. Be careful: the list contains some points that the soldiers do not make.

Cochez dans la liste qui suit tout ce que les trois appelés n'aiment pas.

(a) Obeying pointless orders. ☑

(b) Cleaning the toilets. ☐

(c) Cleaning places they don't make dirty themselves. ☑

(d) Having to do things at fixed times. ☑

(e) The food. ☐

(f) Having to go to bed early. ☐

(g) Getting up early in the morning. ☑

(h) The military hierarchy. ☑

(i) The noise made by other conscripts. ☐

Pour vous aider

avoir à to be obliged to

les corvées fatigue duties (generally, *une corvée* is a chore)

nettoyer to clean

les grades the ranks

au rassemblement on parade

une contrainte à laquelle on a du mal à s'habituer a restriction we find it difficult to get used to

2   In most of these interviews, the key expression used to show dislike is *je n'aime pas*. Towards the end of the sequence, however, Stéphane uses a different expression to indicate a more intense dislike: what is this expression?

Vers la fin de cette séquence, Stéphane utilise une expression qui signifie 'Je déteste'. Qu'elle-est elle?

Expressing dislikes

As we have just seen, the easiest way to express dislike is to say *je n'aime pas*. If you want to express your dislike more strongly, you can use the verb *détester* or the expression *j'ai horreur de*.

You may remember from Section 1 the expressions *c'est supportable* (it's bearable) and *c'est insupportable* (it's unbearable). There is a corresponding verb *supporter*, so to say you can't stand doing something, you can use the expression *je ne supporte pas*. For example, Olivier might have said something like *je ne supporte pas la hiérarchie militaire*.

There will be a chance for further practice in expressing likes and dislikes later in this section.

2.3 Le bon parcours

Whatever apprehensions the conscripts may have when they arrive at the barracks to start their service, they know there will be plenty of physical activity. In the next video sequence you will see *le parcours d'obstacles* and find out whether the conscripts enjoy this kind of strenuous exercise. The video sequence ends with a summing-up of what the conscripts gain from their ten months, or *petite année* (short year). In fact, at the time of filming, the ten months weren't quite up, so the question is in the future tense: *Quand ils repartiront dans la vie civile, qu'est-ce qu'ils emporteront de leur petite année?* (When they go back to civilian life, what will they take away with them from their year?)

Activité 36

3 5   M I N U T E S

1   Read the questions overleaf. Then watch the video (48:02–52:00) and answer the questions by choosing the most appropriate alternative. If you are unsure of your answers, watch the video sequence a second time.

Lisez les questions qui suivent. Ensuite, visionnez la séquence vidéo et choisissez la bonne réponse pour chaque question. Si vous hésitez sur les réponses à donner, regardez la vidéo une deuxième fois.

(a) Stéphane déclare:

    (i) apprécier le parcours d'obstacles;

    (ii) détester le parcours d'obstacles.

(b) Choisissez l'image qui correspond à l'expression 'le passage de l'échelle à corde'.

(c) Choisissez l'image qui correspond à l'expression 'ramper sous les barbelés'.

(d) La plupart des conscrits du 21ème Régiment ont une opinion de la vie militaire:

    (i) négative;

    (ii) positive;

    (iii) très positive.

(e) À la fin des dix mois, ils sont:

    (i) en mauvaise forme physique;

    (ii) en meilleure forme physique.

(f) Ils ont appris des compétences:

(i) utiles;

(ii) nouvelles.

(g) Éric parle des:

(i) mauvais moments qu'il a vécus pendant son service;

(ii) bons moments qu'il a vécus pendant son service.

Pour vous aider

au départ in the beginning

dans la mesure où in so far as

enchaîner to link

essoufflé out of breath

les deux tiers two-thirds

2   Now read the following summaries of what Stéphane, Christophe and Éric say. Some of the information is incorrect. Watch the video sequence (48:02–52:00) again to check and then in French correct the summaries.

Lisez ci-dessous les résumés de ce qu'ont dit Stéphane, Christophe et Éric. Il y a des erreurs. Regardez la séquence vidéo encore une fois pour vérifier. Ensuite corrigez en français les résumés suivants.

(a) Stéphane a découvert de nouveaux sports collectifs qu'il ne connaissait pas avant, mais il trouve toujours très difficile le parcours d'obstacles.

(b) Christophe aime seulement les sports individuels. Ce qui est intéressant pour lui dans le parcours d'obstacles, c'est de pouvoir le faire du début jusqu'à la fin. Il déteste le passage de l'échelle à corde.

(c) Pour Éric, les souvenirs importants de cette petite année, ce sont les amis qu'il a connus et les bons moments qu'il a vécus, mais malheureusement il n'a pas pu passer son permis de conduire.

Activité 37
15 MINUTES
VIDEO

Now watch the last two video sequences (46:52–52:00) again and listen for the various expressions Stéphane, Christophe, Éric and Olivier use to express likes and dislikes. From the list of possibilities below, tick only the expressions they use.

Maintenant regardez à nouveau les deux dernières séquences vidéo en faisant attention aux expressions utilisées pour parler de ce qu'on aime et de ce qu'on n'aime pas. Cochez-les dans la liste ci-dessous quand vous les entendez.

1   Je n'aime pas

2   J'aime particulièrement

3   J'apprécie de   ❑

4   Je déteste   ❑

5   Je ne l'appréciais pas trop   ☑

6   J'ai horreur de   ☑

7   Je n'aime pas beaucoup   ❑

8   J'aime bien   ☑

9   Je ne peux pas supporter   ❑

10 J'adore   ❑

11 C'est insupportable   ❑

12 C'est super   ❑

13 C'est pénible   — hard, tiresome.   ❑

14 C'est désagréable   ❑

15 C'est plutôt agréable   ❑

16 C'est très intéressant   ❑

17 Ça me plaît beaucoup   ❑

18 Ça ne me plaît pas   ❑

Je ne supporte pas

Expressing likes and dislikes

You can see from the list in *Activité 37* that there are a great many ways of expressing likes and dislikes.

You can make a comment using *c'est* + adjective:

> c'est très intéressant

You can also use the verb *plaire*:

> ça me plaît/ça ne me plaît pas

The perfect tense for these expressions is:

> ça m'a plu/ça ne m'a pas plu

Then there is a whole range of verbs. For example:

> aimer, adorer, détester

You can qualify these verbs by adding adverbs like:

> particulièrement, beaucoup, bien

In the next *activité* you'll practise using a variety of ways to express likes and dislikes.

Activité 38
15 MINUTES

1 Listen to the first part of the audio extract. This is a brief dialogue where Mélanie asks Fabien four questions about whether he likes or dislikes certain things. Concentrate on Fabien's replies, as you will be asked to take his role in the second part of the *activité*. You could make notes to help you. The *corrigé* gives you his lines.

Écoutez les quatre questions et réponses. Prenez des notes si vous en avez besoin.

2 In the second part of the audio extract, you will hear the same dialogue, but Fabien's part has been erased. Your task is to answer in his place.

Répondez pendant les pauses, en prenant le rôle de Fabien.

The following *activité* contains an imaginary account of one man's *service militaire*. It will give you further practice in distinguishing between the perfect and imperfect tenses. You may want to refer back to the explanation of this point in Section 1 before you start.

Activité 39
15 MINUTES

In the passage below the verbs in brackets are in the infinitive. Put them into the perfect or imperfect tense, as appropriate. You will have to position *ne* and *pas* correctly, where necessary, and you may have to change *je* to *j'* or *me* to *m'*.

Dans le texte ci-dessous, les verbes entre parenthèses sont à l'infinitif. Mettez-les au passé composé ou à l'imparfait selon le cas.

En 1980 je (passer) mon bac, mais je (ne pas le réussir). Il faut dire qu'à cette époque je (ne pas travailler) beaucoup! Je (aller) tous les soirs au café avec des copains et je (étudier) très peu. Je (avoir) dix-huit ans et pas envie de trouver un emploi. Je (ne pas vouloir) continuer l'école, non plus. Les études, autrefois, ça ne me (plaire) pas tellement. C'est à ce moment-là que je (commencer) mon service militaire.

Au début, ça a été très dur, parce que je ne (connaître) personne. Tous les jours on (faire) des marches de vingt, vingt-cinq kilomètres, ou du parcours d'obstacles, et quand je (être) jeune, je (détester) faire des efforts physiques. Et puis ça (changer): je (faire) la connaissance de types très sympa, je (pouvoir) passer mon permis de conduire, je (vivre) de vraiment bons moments. Finalement, j'ai de très bons souvenirs de mon service militaire.

The final *activité* will help you revise the main points covered in this section. This is a good opportunity for a piece of more extended writing in French, using some of the language and structures you have met so far in this book. Remember to choose the present, perfect or imperfect tense, as appropriate.

Activité 40
4 5   M I N U T E S

Look back over your learning of French in the last few months. Think about how you felt in the first few days when you started this course, what your doubts and difficulties were, what you have liked and not liked – in short, sum up the experience as Éric did on the video. Below are some ideas of the sorts of expression that you might like to use. Aim to write between 100 and 200 words.

Et vous et votre petit trimestre d'apprentissage du français? Qu'est-ce que vous avez appris? Où étaient les difficultés? Vous allez écrire un résumé de vos expériences personnelles, en vous inspirant des expressions indiquées ci-dessous. Essayez d'écrire entre 100 et 200 mots.

Suggestions for your writing

The first few days	au début
	se sentir seul
	connaître
	j'étais
Problems	le plus difficile, c'était
	avoir du mal à
	avoir besoin de
	trouver que
	je crois que
What you liked	rencontrer
	discuter
	apprendre
	en général
	arriver à
	passer de bons moments
What you didn't like	le plus dur
	le plus difficile
	avoir horreur de
Summing up	je regrette que
	je trouve que
	finalement
	j'ai appris
	faire des progrès
	suivre un cours de français
	plus … plus/moins … moins

Obviously, everyone will write different things for this *activité*. We have provided one possible version in the *corrigé*.

Faites le bilan

When you have finished this section of the book, you should be able to:

- Pronounce the sound [sj] intelligibly (*Activité 25*).

- Make comparisons in writing, using the adjective *même* (*Activité 30*).

- Use and understand the expression *arriver à* (*Activité 32*).

- Express your needs using the expression *j'ai besoin de* (*Activité 33*).

- Narrate past events in writing using appropriate past tenses (*Activité 34*).

- Choose accurately between the perfect and imperfect tense when writing (*Activité 39*).

- Express likes and dislikes using the expressions listed on pages 47–8 (*Activité 38*).

Vocabulaire à retenir

2.1 Le service national

un appelé

un conscrit

un objecteur de conscience

outre-mer

un chercheur, une chercheuse

un enseignant, une enseignante

un ingénieur

un état étranger/l'état

faire des études de médecine

2.2 La vie de caserne

la caserne

obtenir le permis de conduire

enrichissant, e

un milieu social

une amitié

un niveau d'études/avoir le même niveau d'études

nous avons/n'avons pas les mêmes goûts

passer de bons moments

faire un petit/gros effort

être tranquille

plaisanter

être seul

jouer au billard

nettoyer

salir

avoir du mal à faire quelque chose

pénible

2.3 Le bon parcours

repartir

emporter

au départ

une compétence

la vie civile

un sport collectif

3 À la prison

STUDY CHART

	Topic	Activity/timing	Audio/video	Key points
2 hrs 5 mins	*3.1 La vie des détenues*	41 (25 mins)		Vocabulary: services available to prisoners
		42 (20 mins)		Vocabulary: masculine and feminine forms of job titles
		43 (15 mins)	Audio	Talking about days and times when activities take place
		44 (10 mins)	Audio	Introduction to the use of *tu* and *vous*
		45 (10 mins)	Audio	Vocabulary: what prison officers and prisoners may and may not do
		46 (10 mins)		
		47 (15 mins)	Audio	Telling people what they may and may not do
1 hr 45 mins	*3.2 Le courrier*	48 (15 mins)	Audio	Vocabulary: censorship of mail in prison
		49 (15 mins)	Audio	
		50 (25 mins)		Using the perfect and imperfect
		51 (20 mins)		Expressing and justifying a point of view
		52 (10 mins)	Audio	Vocabulary: a prisoner's complaint about mail censorship
		53 (15 mins)	Audio	Complaining about work conditions

52

Topic	Activity/timing	Audio/video	Key points
3.3 Les filles qui craquent	54 (15 mins)		Vocabulary: health services
	55 (10 mins)		Vocabulary: nouns and verbs
	56 (10 mins)	Audio	Vocabulary: health professionals working in the prison
	57 (10 mins)	Audio	Vocabulary: how prisoners help each other
	58 (5 mins)		Vocabulary: adjectives describing character
	59 (40 mins)		Section revision

1 hr 35 mins

This section focuses on life in another *collectivité* – a women's prison which is part of the Centre Pénitentiaire de Nantes. You will hear interviews with both a prisoner (*une détenue*) and a prison officer (*une surveillante*) and will read some information handouts for prisoners. The emphasis in the first topic, *La vie des détenues,* is on rules and routine activities. In the second topic, *Le courrier*, you will hear both sides of the argument on the controversial issue of prisoners' mail and whether it should be read by the prison officers. This will give you the opportunity to consolidate your command of constructions used to express constraint and obligation and to extend your range of expressions for putting over a point of view. In the third topic, *Les filles qui craquent,* you will hear about the psychological difficulties some prisoners experience and what help is provided for them. Here you'll come across some health-related vocabulary and have a go at understanding an official prison document. Finally, there will be a chance to practise the perfect/imperfect tense distinction again.

The Feature Cassette that accompanies this book is set in the prison and provides more information about it. Try to listen to this cassette while you are working on this section.

3.1 La vie des détenues

We start by looking at the kinds of activity which are organized for the prison inmates and listen to a prison officer and a prisoner discussing the rules that have to be observed as part of prison routine.

Activités culturelles et sportives

The Centre Pénitentiaire offers various educational and recreational activities. The text *Activités culturelles et sportives* is an information sheet supplied to the prisoners, giving details of some of these activities. This is the kind of text which can be scanned fairly quickly in order to find specific information and one where unfamiliar expressions can normally be guessed from the context. It can also be skimmed for useful vocabulary.

Activité 41

25 MINUTES

1   Scan the text *Activités culturelles et sportives* and indicate whether the following statements are true or false. Correct any false information.

Parcourez le texte 'Activités culturelles et sportives' et indiquez si les phrases ci-dessous sont vraies ou fausses. Corrigez les fausses.

	Vrai	**Faux**
(a) Prison inmates can have their hair done every other Friday morning.	❑	❑
(b) There are sports activities offered on Thursday mornings.	❑	❑
(c) Handicraft classes are given by prison visitors on three afternoons a week.	❑	❑
(d) A beautician offers free beauty treatment once a week.	❑	❑
(e) If they want beauty treatment, inmates have to sign up with the prison officers.	❑	❑
(f) There are drama classes every Thursday, but inmates have to pay for them.	❑	❑
(g) There is a discussion group on Tuesdays.	❑	❑

2   Now skim through the text to find the French for the following jobs.

Trouvez dans le texte l'équivalent français des expressions suivantes.

(a) an actress

(b) a sports instructor

(c) a prison visitor

(d) a beautician

(e) a prison officer

(f) a hairdresser

(g) a teacher

ACTIVITES CULTURELLES ET SPORTIVES

LE SPORT

Un moniteur de sport intervient le mercredi et vendredi de 14h00 à 16h00.

Le mardi de 16h45 à 17h45 cours de yoga.

TRAVAUX MANUELS

Le mardi de 9h00 à 11h30. Le mercredi de 17h00 à 17h45. Le jeudi de 15h00 à 17h00.

Animés par des visiteuses.

PAROLES DE FEMMES

Groupe de parole animé par une visiteuse le lundi de 17h00 à 17h45.

AUDIO VISUEL

Le vendredi de 13h30 à 16h00. Animé par une intervenante extérieure.

THEATRE

Le jeudi de 16h00 à 17h45. Animé par une comédienne.

COIFFURE

Une coiffeuse intervient tous les 15 jours le vendredi de 9h00 à 11h30.

S'inscrire auprès des surveillantes.

Une participation modique vous sera demandée selon les soins.

ESTHETIQUE

Une esthéticienne intervient tous les 15 jours.

Le mardi de 14h à 16h30.

S'inscrire auprès des surveillantes.

Une participation modique vous sera demandée selon les soins.

COURS DE SOUTIEN

Des "visiteuses enseignantes" peuvent vous aider dans certaines matières.

Vous adresser à :

**Mme VASSEUR.
(institutrice)**

Masculine and feminine forms of job names

In *Activité 41*, only one of the jobs that you were asked to identify, *un moniteur,* is in the masculine form in the text: all the other expressions refer to women, which is hardly surprising since this is a women's prison! It is fairly straightforward to change the names of jobs from their feminine to their masculine form, and vice versa. It's a question of knowing (or guessing) the right endings to put on the noun.

Activité 42
20 MINUTES

1   If in French a male sports instructor is *un mon**teur***, and a female teacher is *une institut**rice***, what is the French for the following?

Quelle est la traduction française des expressions suivantes?

(a) a male teacher

(b) a female sports instructor

2   Look at the job names you identified in *Activité 41* and you will see *visit-euse, coméd-ienne, surveill-ante, coiff-euse, esthétic-ienne.* Write down their corresponding masculine forms. See if you can guess them without having to consult a dictionary.

Écrivez le masculin des mots suivants.

(a) une visiteuse

(b) une coiffeuse

(c) une esthéticienne

(d) une comédienne

(e) une surveillante

3   Now write the corresponding feminine forms for the words below.

Donnez le féminin des mots suivants.

(a) un boulanger

(b) un musicien

(c) un chercheur

(d) un directeur

(e) un enseignant

en passant » » » »

Instituteur? Professeur? Enseignant? All of these expressions can be translated as 'teacher' in English, but in French primary school teachers are usually referred to as *instituteurs,* while teachers in secondary and higher education are called *professeurs*. In relaxed speech, these terms are often abbreviated to *un(e) instit* and *un(e) prof.* The generic term to cover any member of the teaching profession is *enseignant*. The equivalent of the English word 'professor' is *un professeur titulaire de chaire*. Other academics are *professeurs d'université*. Interestingly enough, *professeur* is the only one of the three terms which doesn't have a feminine form: *une institutrice, une enseignante*, but *un professeur*. When directly addressing a woman teacher, lecturer or professor in a very formal setting, you would have to say *'Madame le professeur'*. Pupils at school say, more simply, *'Madame'*.

Recognizing 'faux-amis'

Look at the following phrases from the text *Les activités culturelles et sportives*:

> Une coiffeuse **intervient** tous les 15 jours.

> **Animé** par des visiteuses.

> Une **participation** modique vous sera demandée.

So far in Books 1 and 2 of *Cadences* you have met pairs of *faux-amis* where the meaning of the English word is very different from that of the French. (There is an example of this in the Study Guide glossary.) The three phrases above all contain words which look identical or similar to English words, but they have a slightly different meaning in the two languages. *Intervient* may look like 'intervene', but expresses something rather different here: it means, in fact, that the hairdresser 'comes in' once a fortnight. Similarly, to say that the discussion group is 'animated' by the prison visitors sounds very odd: *animé par* here means 'led by'. Finally, while *participation* in French can sometimes mean 'participation' in English, the context here suggests some sort of financial participation, in other words 'a contribution'. It is often the context in which you come across a *faux-ami* that allows you to guess its meaning most accurately. It is useful to keep a note in your dossier of these expressions as you come across them – and beware of jumping to the wrong conclusions over a French word which looks like an English one, particularly when the obvious interpretation doesn't quite seem to make sense!

Now that you've looked at *Les activités culturelles et sportives* in some detail, you are going to be asked to use the same kind of information to answer questions in a slightly different context. Most of the questions you will hear are concerned with the times of various activities, so you will also be revising saying numbers out loud. Try to answer the questions spontaneously, rather than stopping the tape and noting down your answers before you record them.

Listen to the audio extract and answer the questions in the gaps that have been left. To do this, you will need to turn back to page 55 so that you can consult the text *Les activités culturelles et sportives*.

Répondez oralement en français aux questions que vous entendez sur votre cassette. Vous devez avoir sous les yeux le texte 'Les activités culturelles et sportives' pour donner des informations correctes.

Les rapports entre les surveillantes et les détenues

In the next two audio extracts you will hear interviews with a prison officer, Mme Desnoës, and then with a prison inmate, Nicole. Mme Desnoës discusses what is acceptable behaviour from the inmates (*les détenues*), while Nicole comments on what the prison officers (*les surveillantes*) may and may not do. Our focus here is on revising expressions for talking about what is allowed and what is not allowed.

1 In this audio extract you will hear Mme Desnoës explain what she feels is most important in the relationship between inmates and prison officers. This can be summed up in one word, which Mme Desnoës uses several times. Listen and identify this key word from the list given below.

Écoutez Mme Desnoës et choisissez dans la liste suivante le mot qui résume le mieux ce qui pour elle est le plus important dans les rapports entre détenues et surveillantes.

(a) la tolérance

(b) la discipline

(c) le respect

(d) la communication

(e) la patience

2 Which form of address – *tu* or *vous* – would you expect inmates to use with the prison officers? Listen again to Mme Desnoës: are inmates allowed to address the prison officers as *tu*?

Les détenues, ont-elles le droit de tutoyer les surveillantes?

Using 'tu' and 'vous'

As you saw in Book 2 of *Cadences*, *le tutoiement* (calling somebody by the friendly *tu* rather then the slightly more formal *vous*) is usually a mark of friendship. However, Mme Desnoës puts *le tutoiement* on the same level as *les insultes*. This helps to explain why *le tutoiement* is not acceptable between inmates and prison officers; it is also considered unacceptable between army officers and conscripts doing their national service. As a mark of familiarity, the *tu* form can be used to insult and belittle, as well as to indicate friendship and informality. Between conscripts themselves, *le tutoiement* would be used as a mark of camaraderie.

So how do you know when to use *tu* (*tutoyer*) and when to use *vous* (*vouvoyer*)? As a general rule, unless you are talking to children, family or very close friends, it is important to use *vous*, even if the situation appears fairly relaxed. In most francophone business situations, the use of *vous* is standard. However, as you become more friendly, a French friend may suggest that you move on to use *tu* by asking the question: *On se tutoie?*

Interestingly, the leaflet for new entrants to Blanche de Castille which you read in Section 1 addressed the reader as *tu* throughout. Clearly, its authors were trying to create a particular atmosphere, with an emphasis on friendly support and guidance. It is not usual, however, for staff in a secondary school to call their pupils *tu* and some people might find the tone of the *La vie à l'internat* leaflet slightly patronising.

Now you've heard from Mme Desnoës, the prison officer, you are going to listen to Nicole, one of the inmates, commenting on what the prison officers are allowed and not allowed to do.

Activité 45

10 MINUTES

AUDIO 17

Listen to the interview with Nicole and indicate which of the following statements are true and which are false. Correct any false ones.

Écoutez l'interview avec Nicole et indiquez si les affirmations ci-dessous sont vraies ou fausses. Corrigez les fausses.

Les surveillantes ont le droit de:

		Vrai	Faux
1	pénétrer dans les cellules des détenues après sept heures du soir;	☐	☑
2	venir parler dans les cellules pendant la journée;	☑	☐
3	prendre le café avec une détenue dans sa cellule.	☐	☑

Activité 46
10 MINUTES

To revise some of the expressions you know for talking about what is allowed and not allowed, use the information you have just heard to complete the following sentences, so that they summarize the rules of the prison. Obviously, there are several possible answers.

Complétez les phrases suivantes pour résumer ce que vous venez d'apprendre sur le règlement au Centre Pénitentiaire de Nantes.

1   Au Centre Pénitentiaire de Nantes, il est interdit de…

2   Il faut…

3   Les surveillantes ne peuvent pas…

4   Les détenues doivent…

Next we want you to revise some of the expressions for talking about obligation that we've covered so far, but this time in speech and in quite a different context from the prison. The setting for the dialogue in the next audio extract is a busy hotel. Working at the reception desk, you end up having to answer all kinds of enquiries from French guests about what may be done when and where. For things that people have to do, use *il faut*.

Activité 47
15 MINUTES

AUDIO 18

Listen to the audio extract. You will hear prompts in English and should give your reply in French in the gaps that have been left.

Écoutez les questions sur la cassette et répondez en français selon les suggestions qui sont données en anglais.

3.2 Le courrier

We now turn to a subject where there is disagreement between the prison officers and the prisoners. It concerns the mail (*le courrier*). The rules allow for prisoners' mail to be read by the prison officers. In the next two *activités* you will hear interviews with one of the prison officers, Mme David, who defends the practice, and then with Nicole, who explains why she finds it unacceptable. In *Activité 48* we want you to try to predict what the interview contains before you listen to it: obviously there is no *corrigé* for this.

Activité 48
15 MINUTES

1 Before you listen to the interviews, try to imagine the likely arguments from both sides. Why might the prison officers defend the practice of reading prisoners' mail? Why might the prisoners themselves resent it? Jot down a few notes in English, or better still in French.

Avant d'écouter les interviews, imaginez les arguments pour et contre. Notez vos idées en anglais, ou mieux en français.

2 Listen to the first interview on Audio Extract 19 to understand the general meaning of what Mme David says.

Écoutez maintenant l'interview de Madame David.

Pour vous aider
nous trions le courrier we sort the mail
violer to infringe
ressentir to feel
leur état d'esprit their state of mind
on relève we pick out
elles parlent d'évasion they talk about escaping
c'est surtout ça qu'on guette that's mainly what we watch out for

Activité 49
15 MINUTES

Now listen to Nicole and then indicate whether the following statements are true or false. Correct any false ones.

Écoutez maintenant l'interview de Nicole et indiquez si les phrases suivantes sont vraies ou fausses. Corrigez les phrases fausses.

		Vrai	Faux
1	Not all the prisoners complain about their letters being read.	❑	❑
2	The fact that the prison officers read Nicole's personal letters makes her embarrassed to write freely.	❑	❑
3	Only outgoing letters are read by the prison officers.	❑	❑
4	According to Nicole, there are certain things the prisoners are not allowed to write about.	❑	❑
5	Letters that contain anything strange or unusual get sent to the prison governor.	❑	❑

Pour vous aider
le vaguemestre prison officer responsible for mail delivery
j'ai honte I feel ashamed
au juge to the magistrate
au procureur to the public prosecutor
n'importe quoi anything (here: just anything)

en passant » » » »

In France *les juges* have a much wider role to play in the criminal justice system than their opposite numbers in Britain or the United States. Apart from judging cases, French judges work in two very specific areas – as *juges d'instruction* or *juges de l'application des peines*. In the early stages of a criminal investigation, it is a *juge d'instruction* (an examining magistrate) who is responsible for gathering the evidence, not the police. Once a sentence has been given, another type of judge, *le juge de l'application des peines*, oversees its implementation and is responsible for examining applications for parole and arrangements for the prisoner's release. When Nicole talks about prisoners' letters being sent to the judge, she is referring to a *juge de l'application des peines*.

» » » »

The next *activité* gives you further practice in distinguishing between the perfect and imperfect tenses and will help you to learn some of the vocabulary you have met in this section.

Activité 50
25 MINUTES

Translate the following text into French. Translate 'the latter' with *ces dernières*, and 'the governor' with *la directrice*. Between 'each time' and 'a depressed woman', French needs a *que* or a *qu'*. You'll have to decide which.

Traduisez ce texte en français.

> In 1993 there were many changes in the Prison des Mandales. For example, in the past the prison officers used to read the mail. They said that it was in order to help the prisoners, because each time a depressed woman spoke about suicide in a letter, the prison officer knew about it immediately and was able to help her. But the prisoners were not happy. They found it intolerable. They also said that the prison officers were too strict. They did not speak much to the prisoners. Furthermore, the prisoners were not able to do any sport because there was no gym.
>
> And then everything changed with the arrival of the new governor. She decided to improve the prisoners' lives. She organized sports activities. There was more contact between prison officers and prisoners. The women even had the right to see a beautician once a week.

Expressing a point of view

Let's look now at some of the expressions that Mme David used in Audio Extract 19 to put forward her point of view about opening prisoners' mail. (You may want to listen to this audio extract again to refresh your memory.)

She starts by stating her opinion very clearly:

>**C'est pas** négatif…

And she adds her reasons for this opinion:

>… **parce qu'**on arrive toujours à savoir des choses par le courrier.

She concedes, however, that this practice could be seen as an infringement of inmates' privacy:

>**Oui, c'est vrai que** c'est un peu violer leur, euh, leur vie privée…

But then follows this up with what she feels is a further justification for the practice:

>… **mais**, bon, euh… on peut ressentir beaucoup de choses par le courrier.

What Mme David is illustrating here is how to construct an argument in simple French. You can do this by using certain key phrases, as shown below:

C'est Ce n'est pas	une bonne idée négatif	**parce que…**
C'est vrai que	c'est un peu violer leur vie privée	**mais…**

From your work so far in this book, you now know quite a bit about military service in France and life in a French boarding school. Should girls be sent away to boarding school? Is military service a good idea? We want you to express your opinion on these subjects, reusing some of Mme David's phrases. These questions are not meant to be taken too seriously; rather they are to give you a focus for expressing a point of view, based on the model you have just looked at.

Activité 51
20 MINUTES

1 Following the model above, construct pairs of sentences expressing an opinion for and then against the issues of boarding schools for girls, and military service. The elements that should make up each pair of sentences are given on the next page in random order.

Suivant le modèle, construisez des phrases à partir des éléments donnés en (a)–(b) à la page suivante. Notez qu'ils sont dans le désordre.

(a) Mettre une fille au pensionnat?

- elle apprend la discipline/après elle est sûre de se faire des amies durables/elle peut se sentir isolée au début/une bonne chose

- c'est souvent très cher/elle a plus de chances de réussir son bac/ elle perd tout contact avec le monde réel/pas une bonne idée

(b) Faire le service militaire?

- les jeunes ont l'impression de perdre leur temps pendant dix mois/ils apprennent la discipline/pas une bonne chose/la plupart du temps ils sont obligés d'obéir à des ordres inutiles

- on rencontre des gens de milieux sociaux différents/une bonne chose/une excellente préparation à la vie professionnelle/il y a beaucoup de contraintes

2   Now make up a couple of sentences of your own, using the model on page 63, to express your own point of view on the following matters.

Et maintenant, à vous. Rédigez deux ou trois phrases selon le modèle présenté pour exprimer votre point de vue sur les questions suivantes.

(a) Faut-il interdire toutes les voitures dans les centres-villes?

(b) Faut-il obliger tout le monde à apprendre une langue étrangère?

Activité 52
1 0   M I N U T E S

A U D I O   2 0

Read the pairs of sentences listed below and then listen again to Audio Extract 20. Tick which sentence in each pair is the one you hear.

Réécoutez l'Extrait 20 pour repérer les expressions utilisées par Nicole.

1   (a) Tout le monde se plaint de ça.   ❏

      (b) Tout le courrier est plein de ça.   ❏

2   (a) On est seules mais on est très proches.   ❏

      (b) C'est la seule chose que je reproche.   ❏

3   (a) Ça vous est déjà arrivé?   ❏

      (b) Le juge est arrivé.   ❏

The dialogue in the next audio extract contains similar expressions to the ones identified in *Activité 52*, but this time they occur in a slightly different context.

Activité 53
1 5 M I N U T E S

Listen to the audio extract, in which two trade union members – Julia and David – are discussing their respective working conditions. Then in English answer the following questions.

Écoutez l'extrait et répondez en anglais aux questions suivantes.

1   What has never happened to either David or Julia?

2   What are the workers in Julia's workshop not allowed to do?

3   Is there agreement over the no-smoking rule?

4   What does everybody complain about?

5   What does Julia think about the canteen?

3.3 Les filles qui craquent

Some women experience psychological breakdown in prison. A verb much used in relaxed spoken French expresses this: *elles craquent*. This topic looks at what help is available at the Centre Pénitentiaire for prisoners who face various psychological and physical problems. To get a general idea of the health and support services available to prisoners, you're going to look at an extract from the prison's information booklet.

La santé

Your work on this text involves scanning for specific information, as opposed to detailed reading. The text can also be used as a resource for vocabulary building. As with the earlier text, *Activités culturelles et sportives*, you will notice that the language of this official written document is somewhat different from that used in informal conversation.

Activité 54
1 5 M I N U T E S

1   Listed below are the names of the four specific services offered to prison inmates. Scan the *Santé* text overleaf and note down in English what kind of health problems you think each service deals with (two of them provide a service to the same client group).

Lisez le texte et notez en anglais le genre de soins médico-psychologiques fournis.

(a) Service de psychiatrie   (c) Le Triangle d'Or

(b) Antenne toxicomanie   (d) Service d'alcoologie

S A N T E

III° SERVICE MEDICO-PSYCHOLOGIQUE

A - Service de psychiatrie

L'équipe de médecins, psychologue et infirmiers(ières), appartenant au Centre Hospitalier de Nantes, assure, à votre demande, la prise en charge psychologique de vos troubles d'ordre nerveux sous forme de consultations individuelles.

Cette équipe peut aussi développer avec vous une réflexion sur vos difficultés personnelles liées ou non à l'incarcération.

Pour demander à être suivie, écrire :

- au Docteur MICHAUD, psychiatre, chef de service,
- ou au Docteur BETBEZE, psychiatre,
- ou à Madame BOQUIEN, psychologue.

B - Antenne toxicomanie

Composée d'une infirmière, d'un psychologue (mi-temps) et d'une assistante sociale (mi-temps), cette équipe, appartenant également au Centre Hospitalier, assure à votre demande la prise en charge de vos difficultés liées à la toxicomanie.

Elle peut vous assurer un suivi médico-psychologique, une information sur les secteurs de soins existants à l'extérieur et préparer votre sortie avec vous.

Pour demander à être suivie, écrire à l'un des membres de l'Antenne.

IV° LE TRIANGLE D'OR

est une consultation pour toxicomanes.

Le Triangle d'Or tente de répondre aux problèmes liés à la toxicomanie.

Il apporte une aide à toutes celles qui en expriment la demande par une démarche volontaire.

Les demandes sont à formuler par l'intermédiaire ou non de l'Antenne Toxicomanie au :

Triangle d'Or
15, rue Crébillon
44000 NANTES

V° SERVICE D'ALCOOLOGIE

Vous pensez avoir un problème avec l'alcool. Vous avez envie de vous informer, d'en parler, d'y réfléchir, de rencontrer quelqu'un.

Vous pouvez écrire :

Centre d'Alcoologie
62, rue Georges Lafont
44300 NANTES

ou formuler votre demande au Service Médico-Psychologique qui transmettra.

Pour vous aider

assure… la prise en charge psychologique de vos troubles d'ordre nerveux ensures that treatment is provided for any psychological problems

liées ou non à related or unrelated to

être suivie to receive treatment

à votre demande at your request

soins treatments

2 Now scan the text to identify the five health-related jobs it mentions. Suggest an English translation for each one.

Trouvez dans le texte cinq professions liées à la santé et traduisez les noms en anglais.

Recognizing different styles within a text

If you look at this text again, you may notice that the style of the section on the Service d'alcoologie comes across as more direct and more informal than the others. It talks directly to the reader with sentences that begin with *vous*. It also uses a lot of verbs:

> Vous **pensez** avoir un problème… Vous **avez envie de** vous **informer**, d'en **parler**, d'y **réfléchir**, de **rencontrer** quelqu'un.

This contrasts with the other three sections, which are more distant and impersonal in tone. One of the key differences lies in the way the sentences are constructed. In Sections IIIe and IVe of the text there are a number of sentences where an idea that would probably be expressed by a single verb in a more relaxed context is expressed instead by a phrase consisting of a verb followed by a noun. It's easier to see the pattern from examples. Here's one from Section IVe.

> Il **apporte une aide** à toutes celles qui en expriment la demande…

In less formal French *il apporte une aide* would probably be replaced by *il aide*. The frequent use of these verb + noun constructions is increasingly characteristic of modern French and, in particular, of the language used in the press and other media.

The nouns used in such constructions often relate to everyday verbs, so to guess what their meaning is it helps to be able to identify families of words. You have already worked along these lines in Section 2. *Activité 55* focuses on finding nouns connected with verbs.

Activité 55
10 MINUTES

Look at the *Santé* text again and find the nouns which correspond to the verbs in the table below.

Trouvez dans le texte les noms qui correspondent aux verbes donnés ci-dessous.

Verbes	Noms
prendre en charge	
réfléchir	
suivre	
sortir	
s'informer	
aider	
consulter	
soigner	

Having looked at the health services provided for prison inmates, we now go back to hear from one of the inmates herself. Nicole was asked to say what happens if one of the prison inmates experiences depression (*la déprime,* informal for *la dépression*) or 'cracks up' (*si l'une d'entre elles craque*). In such cases, a number of professionals become involved. In *Activité 56* you will find out who does what. But to what extent can a fellow prisoner get involved? This is the key question in *Activité 57*. *Activité 58* asks you to describe Nicole's personality.

Activité 56
10 MINUTES

AUDIO 22

1   Read the list below and predict which of these professionals are likely to become involved in cases of nervous breakdown. Then listen to what Nicole has to say on Audio Extract 22 in order to check your answers.

Choisissez dans cette liste les professionnels qui, à votre avis, pourraient prendre en charge les détenues qui ont des problèmes psychologiques. Ensuite, écoutez Nicole pour vérifier votre réponse.

(a) les assistantes sociales

(b) les enseignants

(c) les médecins

(d) les psychologues

(e) la coiffeuse

(f) les surveillantes

(g) les visiteuses

2   Once you have found out who gets involved, identify who does what by filling in the gaps below with the expressions Nicole uses in the interview. You may want to listen to Audio Extract 22 again.

Vous avez déjà une idée des professionnels qui s'occupent des détenues. Vérifiez maintenant les détails données par Nicole en complétant la transcription ci-dessous.

(a) Donc il y a les _____ et les _____ , les
_____ . Alors donc ils essaient, ben de _____ ,
de lui _____ des _____ , pour, euh… le stress, pour,
euh, la déprime.

(b) Les surveillantes _____ _____ _____ parce
que… elles* _____ la _____ en lui, en lui faisant…,
en lui parlant.

* She should have said *parce qu'elles*.

68

Activité 57

10 MINUTES

AUDIO 23

In this audio extract Nicole is asked: *Est-ce que vous avez le droit de demander de prendre dans votre chambre une fille qui craque nerveusement parce que vous avez de bonnes relations avec elle et que vous pourriez l'aider?* Listen to the audio extract and choose which of the alternatives below best summarizes her reply.

Choisissez parmi les phrases suivantes celle qui résume le mieux la réponse de Nicole.

1   No, the prison governor has expressly forbidden it. I had a friend who was feeling suicidal and they wouldn't even let me go to her cell. In the end, she stayed in the hospital for a week.

2   Yes, the prison governor asked me recently to go and spend the night in the same room as a woman who was suicidal. I agreed, so that's what I did for a week and the woman didn't commit suicide.

3   Yes, the prison governor has finally given in to our requests on this. I asked her recently if I could stay with another women who was suicidal and in the end she agreed, but I had to report back to her every morning.

Activité 58

5 MINUTES

Now you have heard her tell this story, what kind of person do you imagine Nicole is? Look at the list of adjectives below and choose those which you feel describe her best.

Vous avez entendu l'histoire que raconte Nicole. Quelle impression avez-vous de sa personnalité? Choisissez parmi la liste d'adjectifs suivante ceux qui la décrivent le mieux.

1   généreuse

2   pessimiste

3   difficile

4   égoïste

5   méfiante

6   chaleureuse

7   compréhensive

8   autoritaire

9   renfermée

10 timide

In this book you have had quite a bit of practice in using the imperfect and the perfect. Here is an opportunity to use them orally to recount on tape some of your own memories – very much along the same lines as the former pupil from Blanche de Castille did in Section 1, *Activité 22*.

You will need to take a bit of time to think through what you're going to say, but it's best not to write out the script of your talk. You are aiming at more or less spontaneous speech. You'll find some guidelines below on what you could talk about, but do feel free to add other details. Although it's as well to practise out loud a couple of times before you record yourself, remember that your aim is to sound as spontaneous as possible. You might like to imagine yourself reminiscing with French friends.

Activité 59
40 MINUTES

Record a short monologue (about one minute long) about a situation from your past – for instance, your routine at school or a job you used to have. You may like to mention the following:

- when you started in that particular establishment;
- what your daily routine was like in those days;
- what you liked and disliked;
- when you left and what you did after leaving.

Bear in mind, too, the distinction between the perfect and imperfect tenses.

Enregistrez un petit exposé d'une minute où vous vous rappelez une période de votre passé, peut-être vos études ou un travail.

Faites le bilan

When you have finished this section of the book, you should be able to:

- Understand some of the patterns for masculine and feminine endings (*Activité 42*).
- Use *le* with the name of a day of the week to say when something happens (*Activité 43*).
- Understand some aspects of the use of *tu* and *vous* (*Activité 44*).
- Translate the English past tense accurately into the French perfect or imperfect tenses (*Activité 50*).
- Express and justify a point of view using the phrases *c'est... parce que...* and *c'est vrai que... mais...* (*Activité 51*).

Vocabulaire à retenir

3.1 *La vie des détenues*

un détenu, une détenue

un surveillant, une surveillante

intervenir

animer

un groupe

une soirée

une participation

un atelier de théâtre

un coiffeur, une coiffeuse

un comédien, une comédienne

un moniteur, une monitrice

un instituteur, une institutrice

3.2 *Le courrier*

le courrier

ressentir

un état d'esprit

la vie privée

se plaindre (de quelque chose)

reprocher quelque chose à quelqu'un

bizarre

n'importe quoi

avoir honte

3.3 *Les filles qui craquent*

lié,e à

un assistant social, une assistante sociale

un toxicomane, une toxicomane

la toxicomanie

formuler une demande

un médecin

un infirmier, une infirmière

un psychologue, une psychologue

un psychiatre, une psychiatre

s'informer

soigner

les soins (mpl)

une dépression

être déprimé

le stress

être stressé

se suicider

un médicament

craquer

4 Au monastère

This section gives you a chance to evaluate how well you are working with the video material. Although this is an optional section, you'll find you'll derive a lot of benefit from it if you do decide to do it.

We want you to watch a short video sequence (52:07–65:15). It was filmed at the Abbaye de Melleray near Nantes and you will listen to two of the Trappist monks there talking about monastic life. The focus of what they say is very similar to that in the rest of this book: for example, they too talk about the things that they like about their life style and the constraints that it imposes on them.

At this point in the course, you should treat the viewing of this short documentary video as an opportunity to reflect upon your language learning strategies, i.e. the sorts of activities, techniques and approaches that you find most effective in helping you to grasp what is being said. It is important to think about this because choosing the right strategy will help you to retain and ultimately to produce the words and expressions that you consider important when writing or speaking the language.

Here are some techniques you can try out when working with video material:

- Remember to make use of the Transcript Booklet. You can refer to this whenever you feel the need, though the transcript should not be your starting-point. Watch the video first!

- When you're trying to understand what is being talked about on the video, make use of what you already know. Therefore at each stage of viewing try to predict some of the vocabulary that will be used. For example, you know that the video sequence you're going to watch next is on the subject of the monastic life. You could prepare yourself by listing some of the words you think might be included: what are the French words for 'monks', 'prayer', 'a monastery', etc? Look up the words in the dictionary if you don't know them and then listen out for them on the sound-track. You may also be able to predict some of the ideas contained in the video – you will be surprised how often a few inspired guesses before watching can help you with the language that is used.

- Watch each video sequence all the way through a first time in order to get a general impression. At this stage in learning another language, you will probably be relying to quite an extent on the images presented in order to grasp the content.

- Then watch the sequence all the way through again. This time you could think about the overall structure. You will find that the video can be split into several sections. Visual clues such as text on the screen, different people speaking and the setting in which you see them can be used as indications of the separate sections. Don't worry if you can't catch everything that's said – the monks do not always express themselves with total clarity!

- If you feel that you have enough information at this stage, you could note down your initial ideas on each section. These notes could include, for example, what you think the main topic of the conversation or interview is. Add any details you think you have grasped: these may be individual words or expressions in French, or more general jottings of points to watch out for next time.

- Next, concentrate on specific sections of the video, perhaps starting with the bits you think you find easiest to understand. Add to your notes on the section, perhaps expanding individual words into phrases. Remember that *you* control the video recorder! The machine has STOP, PAUSE and REWIND buttons: use them as much as you like. You should find that each successive replaying of a particular section will reveal more of the language used.

You could also ask yourself the following questions in order to clarify in your own mind what strategies are most appropriate for you:

- What do I want to learn from this video: for example, do I want to increase my level of comprehension of natural spoken French, find out information about life in France, learn specific words and phrases, improve my pronunciation and intonation?

- What are the difficulties involved in achieving my learning objectives: for example, lack of clarity, speed of speaking, insufficient visual clues, insufficient knowledge of specialized vocabulary?

- What aspects of the video can help me to increase my level of comprehension: for example, picking up background visual clues, seeing the mouths of the speakers, repetition of phrases by the speakers, use of simple vocabulary?

- What techniques do I find most useful to adopt: for example, watching and listening for gist, pausing and repeating, rewinding the video recorder and replaying short sections of the video material, noting down words and phrases?

Thinking about these questions should give you a clearer idea of the strategies that are most useful to you when watching a video. These strategies will obviously vary according to the difficulty of the language used and the type of material; nevertheless, you should try to apply your findings to other video sequences later in the course.

Viewing guide

If you have time to work on the *Au monastère* video sequence in a bit more depth, or would simply like to confirm some of the things that you have worked out from your independent viewing, we have provided brief summaries of each section of this video sequence with a list of useful vocabulary.

Les moines de Melleray

(52:07–60:14)

The first section of the video introduces the abbey at Melleray and the community of Trappist monks who live there. In particular, we see one of the monks (*le Frère Marc*) who is in charge of the financial side of things and the abbot (*le Père Abbé*) who leads the order. These two monks form the basis of the documentary that follows.

> ***Pour vous aider***
>
> *à l'écart du monde*   away from the world
>
> *plusieurs offices*   several religious services
>
> *doivent faire face aux soucis d'argent*   must confront money worries
>
> *une hôtellerie*   a hotel (here, a visitors' residential building)

Dans le parc, un panneau demande le silence

In the first interview Brother Marc talks about how the monks get up for an early morning service at 4 a.m. and how this enables them to think about and pray for people whose suffering or trials keep them awake. He goes on to describe how the times of their waking and sleeping mean that the monks are 'out of phase' with modern life.

Pour vous aider

qui sont éveillées par la souffrance   whose suffering keeps them awake

l'épreuve   hardship

nous nous solidarisons donc avec   we feel solidarity therefore with

en priant   by praying

décalée   out of phase

The abbot explains that the monks' life resembles family life, in which each individual must play a part.

Pour vous aider

moyennant   taking into account

qui répartit   who allocates

Meal-times play an important role in the life of the community. Meals are conducted in silence. The abbot explains what the monks may and may not eat and drink.

Pour vous aider

ils se réunissent   they meet

autorise   allows

la boisson du pays   the locally produced drink

une lecture   a reading (of a religious text)

ne comporte pas de   does not include any

uniquement   solely

laitages   dairy products

Brother Marc, whom you may remember talked about his favourite leisure pursuits at the beginning of Book 2 of *Cadences*, explains how even within the ordered monastic life it is possible to have one's own personal routine. Here he tells us a bit more about the sorts of thing that he likes to do with the relatively large amount of free time that he enjoys.

Pour vous aider

à telle heure   at such and such a time

en dehors des temps prescrits   outside the set times

Qu'est-ce qui vous plaît dans ce style de vie?

(60:18–61:08)

When asked what it is that the monks like about the life they lead, Brother Marc mentions the balance of things that make up a monk's day. The abbot says that in the thirty-seven years that he has been there he has found a meaning to his life.

> **Pour vous aider**
>
> *l'équilibre*   the balance
>
> *un sens*   a meaning

Le Frère Marc et le Père Abbé

Et les contraintes?

(61:09–62:30)

When asked about the constraints that their way of life imposes on them, Brother Marc first mentions the fact that the monks live most of their life in silence. He then speaks of the asceticism that is required of them when they first arrive at the monastery. He explains that they have to learn to control their sensitivity, their ambition and their jealousy. Finally, he says that by making sure their minds are empty of personal ambitions, and by not seeking their own individual well-being but rather that of others, they do mysteriously find happiness.

Pour vous aider

une grosse ascèse   a big effort towards asceticism

maîtriser   to control

la sensibilité   sensitivity

la jalousie   jealousy

ceux qui nous entourent   those around us

nous ne gardons rien   we keep nothing

Les business-moines

(62:33–65:15)

This section looks at how, over the centuries, the monks have interpreted the requirement that they earn their own living. This has led them from producing illuminated manuscripts, through agriculture, to today's work of desktop publishing.

Pour vous aider

de magnifiques enluminures   beautiful illuminations (on a manuscript)

nous nous sommes aperçus... que   we realized ... that

les religieux   monks

nous avons dû nous orienter alors vers   we then had to turn towards

des appareils   equipment

la concurrence   the competition

Corrigés

Section 1

Activité 1

À **sept heures vingt** il faut se réveiller.

À sept heures cinquante il faut **descendre prendre le petit déjeuner**.

À **huit heures trente** il faut aller au premier cours.

À douze heures vingt-cinq il faut **aller déjeuner**.

Activité 2

This is how the exercise should have gone:

- Bon, alors, on va passer la journée à Londres demain, c'est ça? À quelle heure on se lève?
- (You have to get up at six o'clock.)
- Il faut se lever à six heures.
- Oh là, là! C'est tôt! Pour être à la gare à quelle heure?
- (You have to be at the station at seven o'clock.)
- Il faut être à la gare à sept heures.
- Bon, d'accord.

Activité 3

Here is the conversation which you should have had:

- Qu'est-ce qu'on doit faire dans la cuisine avant de partir?
- Il faut nettoyer.
- Et quoi encore?
- Il faut vider la poubelle.
- C'est tout?
- Il faut éteindre le frigo.
- Et ensuite?
- Il faut prendre note du numéro du compteur électrique.
- D'accord, et à part ça?
- Il faut mettre les serviettes sales dans le panier à linge.
- Et quoi encore?
- Il faut faire l'inventaire.
- C'est tout?
- Il faut avertir le propriétaire de notre départ.

Activité 4

1 Souvent l'été, je me lève très tôt et je prends mon petit déjeuner sur le balcon **en regardant** ce qui se passe dans ma rue. Vers sept heures, j'entends le facteur qui descend la rue **en chantant**. Heureusement qu'il a une belle voix! Quand il passe devant ma fenêtre, il me donne mon courrier **en me disant** 'Encore des lettres d'amour pour vous, Mademoiselle Fournier?' Ensuite, je vois mon voisin, Monsieur Prost, qui part **en courant** vers la gare. Il est toujours en retard! Il oublie toujours quelque chose. Et puis vers huit heures moins dix, j'entends des portes claquer. Ce sont les enfants qui partent à l'école **en criant** et **en se bousculant**, leur cartable sur le dos.

2 Here is a rough translation of the passage. Your own translation may have differed slightly, but make sure that your translations of *en* + present participle have the same meaning as those given here.

> Often in the summer I get up very early and have my breakfast on the balcony **while watching** what is going on in my street. At about seven o'clock I hear the postman **singing** as he comes down the street. Fortunately he has a nice voice! When he comes past my window he gives me my post, **saying to me** 'More love letters for you, Miss Fournier?' Then I see my neighbour, Mr Prost, leaving **at a run** for the station. He is always late! He always forgets something. And then at about ten to eight, I hear doors slamming. It's the children leaving for school with their satchels on their backs, **shouting out** and **jostling one another**.

Activité 5

1 (a) Après le déjeuner, nous avons les cours normaux de l'après-midi et une petite récréation.

(b) Ensuite, nous avons l'étude.

(c) Après l'étude, à sept heures quinze, nous allons dîner.

(d) En général, à huit heures moins le quart, nous remontons dans nos chambres.

(e) Entre sept heures quarante-cinq et neuf heures, nous pouvons écouter de la musique.

2 (a) Les jeunes filles doivent travailler pendant l'étude, c'est-à-dire avant le dîner.

(b) Pendant l'autre période non surveillée, c'est-à-dire entre huit heures moins le quart et neuf heures, elles ont le droit d'aller les unes chez les autres pour discuter et pour écouter de la musique.

(Do you remember this use of *pour* to state a purpose? You first saw it in *Cadences*, Book 2, Section 3.)

Activité 6

Ensuite nous avons l'étude qui n'est pas surveillée, c'est-à-dire que chacune d'entre nous reste dans sa chambre, pour travailler; mais, euh…, donc **c'est interdit** d'aller les unes chez les autres car ça les empêche de travailler.

En général, à huit heures moins le quart nous avons terminé de dîner, nous remontons dans nos chambres et… et là **on a le droit** d'aller chacune les unes chez les autres.

Activité 7

1 Dans les cinémas en Grande-Bretagne et en France, vous n'avez pas le droit de fumer.

2 Dans beaucoup de musées français, il est interdit de prendre des photos.

3 Dans beaucoup de forêts françaises, le camping est interdit.

4 En Grande-Bretagne, les commerces ont le droit d'ouvrir le dimanche.

5 Dans les pubs anglais, seules les personnes de plus de dix-huit ans ont le droit de consommer des boissons alcoolisées. (You could also have said *'ont le droit de boire de l'alcool'.*)

6 Sur beaucoup de plages en France, les chiens sont interdits.

Activité 8

1 Here are the sorts of notes you should have made (although you may have used slightly different phrases).

(a) Selon Fabienne et Anne-Catherine, les jeunes filles sont réveillées à sept heures vingt: selon le texte, elles sont réveillées à sept heures quinze.

(b) Selon Fabienne et Anne-Catherine, il faut descendre prendre le petit déjeuner à huit heures moins dix: selon le texte, il faut descendre à huit heures moins le quart.

(c) Selon Fabienne et Anne-Catherine, le premier cours est à huit heures et demie: selon le texte, les cours commencent à huit heures dix.

(d) Selon Fabienne et Anne-Catherine, la récréation l'après-midi est d'un quart d'heure: selon le texte, la récréation est d'une demi-heure.

(e) Selon Fabienne et Anne-Catherine, les jeunes filles ont le droit de discuter dans leurs chambres après le repas du soir: selon le texte, elles sont obligées de respecter toujours le silence.

2 (a) Tu fais ta toilette (infinitive: faire sa toilette).

(b) Tu ranges ta chambre (infinitive: ranger sa chambre).

(c) N'oublie pas tes affaires.

(d) Tu peux te détendre.

(e) Voir les informations à la télévision. (Note that *actualités* is a synonym for *les infos*, which you met in Book 2 of *Cadences*.)

Activité 9

On (ne) peut pas:

1 **Regarder la télévision** aussi souvent que chez soi.

2 **Laisser la lumière allumée** tard le soir, lire donc très longtemps.

On est obligé(es) de:

3 **Penser** aux autres.

Activité 10

1 (a) **Il est interdit d'**écouter de la musique après vingt et une heures.

(b) **On ne peut pas** laisser la lumière allumée après vingt et une heures trente.

(c) **Il ne faut pas** courir dans les couloirs.

(d) **On est obligé(e) de** se lever à sept heures vingt.

(e) **On doit** travailler en silence pendant l'étude.

(f) **On a le droit de** regarder la télévision une fois par semaine.

2 Here are some possible sentences. Check that you have used the infinitive form of the verb after the expressions given, as in the examples below.

(a) À midi, je suis obligé(e) de **manger** dans un restaurant, parce qu'il n'y a pas de cantine là où je travaille.

(b) À la bibliothèque municipale, je n'ai pas le droit d'**emprunter** des livres: j'ai seulement le droit de les **consulter** sur place.

(c) Au travail, il est interdit de **fumer**.

(d) Je ne peux pas **inviter** des amis parce que je n'ai pas assez de place chez moi.

(e) Je dois **aller** à Bruxelles deux fois par mois pour mon travail.

Activité 11

Fabienne starts off by saying *'ça me plaît beaucoup'* (I like it a lot) and finishes with *'c'est supportable'* (it's bearable). On balance, the impression is that she is fairly happy at Blanche de Castille.

Activité 13

This is how the dialogue should have gone:

– Dites-moi, vous venez de changer d'emploi, n'est-ce pas? Votre nouvel emploi là, à Londres, comment ça va?

– (You like it a lot, it's very motivating.)

– Ça me plaît beaucoup, c'est très motivant.

– C'est pas trop difficile de travailler à plusieurs dans le même bureau?

– (Well, it's bearable.)

– Eh bien… c'est supportable…

– Et vous y allez en train tous les matins?

– (Yes, that's right and you don't like it at all.)

– Oui, c'est ça…et ça ne me plaît pas du tout!

– Je comprends. Et le matin, j'imagine qu'il y a beaucoup de monde dans les trains…

– (Yes, it's unbearable.)

– Oui… c'est insupportable!

– Et oui… elle est difficile, la vie! Paris, c'est la même chose… je suis obligée de me lever vers cinq heures et demie maintenant pour arriver à l'heure au travail… Soit il n'y a pas de place dans les trains, soit les trains sont en retard, etc. etc…

Activité 14

1 (a) 1 Les professeurs sont assez motivants, ils s'intéressent à nous et à nos problèmes (scolaires ou familiaux) (they are interested in the pupils and concerned with both school and home).

 (b) 2 and 6 Des ordinateurs, un labo de langues et une grande salle de sport (computers, a language laboratory and a large sports hall); cadre agréable avec un grand parc (pleasant surroundings with extensive grounds).

 (c) 4 and 7 Il y a beaucoup de sorties et de voyages culturels et linguistiques (there are a lot of outings and cultural and language trips); école dynamique car elle participe à des concours et organise des activités sportives (a dynamic school because it takes part in competitions and organizes sporting activities).

 (d) 8 Les responsables de l'établissement assurent une bonne discipline et fixent des règles à respecter (the people who run the school make sure that discipline is good and establish rules that must be adhered to).

2 The only negative point is 3, where the writer says that the atmosphere among the girls is not always very good, which she puts down to the fact that there aren't enough boys (*il n'y a pas assez de garçons*).

3 (a) Ils s'intéressent à nos problèmes.

 (b) Des ordinateurs.

 (c) L'ambiance.

 (d) Sorties.

 (e) Cadre agréable.

 (f) Elle (l'école) participe à des concours.

 (g) Des règles à respecter.

Activité 15

2 Les études

 (c) This is what Anne-Catherine actually says: '*en entrant ici on est presque, pratiquement sûre d'avoir son bac et…, et déjà la réputation de Blanche de Castille devrait nous ouvrir des portes après pour des études supérieures*'.

 Les amies

 (e) This is what Fabienne actually says: '*Je pense que, à Blanche, plus on monte dans les classes, plus on vieillit, plus on mûrit, plus on se fait des amies durables, des véritables amies*'.

Activité 16

1 Here is one way of matching the phrases:

 (a) Plus on fixe de règles, moins les gens les respectent.

 (b) Plus je lis d'œuvres philosophiques, moins je m'intéresse à la philosophie.

 (c) Plus on fait de sport, plus on se détend.

(d) Plus on sort, plus on se fait d'amis.

(e) Moins je mange, moins j'ai envie de manger.

(f) Plus on regarde les informations à la télévision, plus on se sent impuissant face aux problèmes du monde.

But you may have thought that (c) and (d) could be as follows:

(c) Plus on fait de sport, plus on se fait d'amis.

(d) Plus on sort, plus on se détend.

2 Here are some suggestions of the sort of sentences you might have written:

(a) Plus on vieillit, plus on apprécie le calme.

(b) Moins on travaille, plus on peut faire de sport.

(c) Plus on étudie la grammaire française, moins on fait d'erreurs!

(d) Moins on parle, plus les gens vous écoutent.

Activité 17

Here are the questions and answers which you should have recorded:

– Comment est-ce qu'on réussit aux examens?

– (By working hard.)

– En travaillant dur.

– Comment est-ce qu'on peut se détendre après une journée de travail?

– (By doing some regular sport.)

– En pratiquant un sport régulièrement.

– (Or by watching television.)

– Ou en regardant la télévision.

– Comment peut-on apprendre à se servir d'un ordinateur?

– (By reading the manual.)

– En lisant le manuel.

– Comment est-ce qu'on arrive à bien parler français?

– (First of all by following a course.)

– D'abord en suivant des cours.

– (Then by listening often to French radio.)

– Ensuite en écoutant souvent la radio française.

– (And finally by going to live in France.)

– Et finalement, en allant vivre en France.

Activité 18

2 (a) In France children start school at the age of **six** and can leave when they are **sixteen**.

(b) The sixth form in Great Britain corresponds to **la première** and **la terminale** in the French school system.

(c) A pupil who is *en quatrième* is likely to be **thirteen or fourteen** years old.

(d) In the French system pupils who have grave difficulty coping with the syllabus may have to **repeat a year in the same class** (*redoubler*).

(e) The preparation for the *baccalauréat* normally lasts **three** years.

(f) A *boîte à bac* is a French private school which has a reputation for **getting weak pupils through their baccalauréat**.

Activité 20

1 This is how you should have matched the expressions:

(a) Je voyais des gens pas très fréquentables.

(iii) I used to mix with bad company.

(b) On me menaçait de me mettre en pension.

(v) They threatened to send me to boarding school.

(c) J'ai fait une très mauvaise seconde.

(iv) I did really badly in my fifth year

(d) J'ai cru que tout allait s'écrouler autour de moi.

(ii) I thought everything was going to collapse around me.

(e) Je suis arrivée ici en pleurant.

(vi) I arrived here in tears.

(f) Je suis pas une fille comme il faut.

(i) I'm not a very well brought up young lady.

2 Here are the true and false statements:

(a) Faux. Elle dit 'je travaillais pas à l'école'.

(b) Vrai. Elle dit 'une école très stricte; et pour moi Blanche de Castille c'était vraiment, euh, les bourgeois'.

(c) Faux. Non, elle y est allée après sa seconde. On la menaçait depuis sa sixième de la mettre en pension.

(d) Faux. Elle dit 'Je suis arrivée ici en pleurant, "Je vous prie, ne m'acceptez pas."' (Note here the use of *en* + present participle to give more detail about how she arrived at the school.)

Activité 21

1 Avant, **j'étais** une jeune fille assez, euh, désolante pour mes parents, selon mes parents. C'est-à-dire que **je sortais** beaucoup, **je voyais** des gens pas très fréquentables et, euh, **je tournais** mal, et **je travaillais pas** à l'école. Depuis la sixième, c'est-à-dire vers dix ans, **on me menaçait** de me mettre en pension à Blanche de Castille, c'est-à-dire une école très stricte; et pour moi, Blanche de Castille **c'était** vraiment, euh, les bourgeois, le..., le style vraiment particulier, d'aristocrates.

2 Donc, j'ai..., **j'ai fait** une très mauvaise seconde, et **on m'a autorisée** à redoubler; et, euh, donc **on m'a dit**: 'Anne-Catherine, tu vas aller en pension à Blanche de Castille.' Alors là, **j'ai cru** que tout allait s'écrouler autour de moi, **c'était** vraiment l'enfer... Et donc **je suis arrivée** ici en pleurant 'Je vous en prie, ne m'acceptez pas, je suis pas une fille comme il

faut'; et finalement, ben, **ils m'ont acceptée** pour justement resserrer la vis.

(Note: ***c'était*** *l'enfer* is in the imperfect because it refers to a description of the situation, not an clearly defined action like the other verbs.)

Activité 22

- Je suis entrée (perfect tense, a completed event).
- L'école était (imperfect tense, description in the past).
- Il n'y avait (imperfect tense, description in the past).
- On portait (imperfect tense, talking about past habits – we used to wear).
- Tout le monde détestait (imperfect tense, description of feelings in the past).
- On se levait (imperfect tense, talking about past habits – we used to get up).
- Il y avait beaucoup de contraintes (imperfect tense, description in the past).
- La discipline était très stricte (imperfect tense, description in the past).
- On n'avait pas le droit de (imperfect tense, description in the past).
- C'était une école très bien équipée (imperfect tense, description in the past).
- Il y avait un laboratoire (imperfect tense, description in the past).
- J'ai passé mon baccalauréat (perfect tense, a completed event).
- Je ne l'ai pas réussi (perfect tense, a completed event). *Ne pas réussir* in this context is an equivalent of the English 'to fail'. 'I failed' is *je ne l'ai pas réussi* and is therefore a completed event.
- J'ai redoublé (perfect tense, a completed event).
- J'ai eu mon bac (perfect tense, a completed event).
- J'ai quitté Blanche de Castille (perfect tense, a completed event).
- J'ai fait un diplôme (perfect tense, a completed event).
- J'ai terminé en 1992 (perfect tense, a completed event).

Section 2

Activité 23

1(a); 2(b); 3(b); 4(a); 5(a).

Activité 24

1

Non-military option	Activities include	Place of work	Length of service
(a) Service de la coopération	Traffic control (c)	France (c) (d)	16 months (a) (b)
	Computing (b)	Other foreign countries (a)	20 months (d)
(b) Aide technique	Engineering (a) (b)		10 months (c)
(c) Police nationale	Research (a) (b)	DOM-TOM (b)	
(d) Objecteur de conscience	Social work (b) (d)		
	Teaching (a) (b)		

2 (a) chercheurs

   (b) enseignants

   (c) ingénieurs

3 (a) Hervé Desforges. Forme civile: le service de la coopération. Durée: 16 mois.

   (b) Jean-Paul Peraud. Forme civile: le service de la coopération/l'aide technique. Durée: 16 mois.

   (c) Alain Latour. Forme civile: objecteur de conscience. Durée: 20 mois.

   (d) Simon Leclerc. Forme civile: l'aide technique. Durée: 16 mois.

Activité 26

Verbe	Nom
circuler	la circulation
enseigner	l'enseignant(e), l'enseignement
servir	le service
demander	la demande
durer	la durée
coopérer	la coopération
développer	le développement
assister	l'assistance
chercher	le chercheur, la chercheuse
accueillir	l'accueil

Activité 27

1 The three items you did not see were:

(b) un avion qui décolle d'un aéroport militaire;

(f) le bureau du commandant;

(i) des conscrits en train de ranger leurs affaires.

2 (a) Faux. En général, le service national se fait à l'âge de dix-huit ans.

(b) Vrai.

(c) Vrai.

(d) Vrai.

(e) Vrai.

(f) Faux. Olivier dit qu'ils ont très peu de moments seuls pendant la journée.

Activité 28

1 Éric; 2 Stéphane; 3 Christophe; 4 Olivier; 5 Éric.

Activité 29

1 Il y a la vie en collectivité, le fait que l'on se retrouve avec des gens que l'on ne connaissait pas du tout, qui sont pas forcément du même **âge** que moi, qui n'ont pas forcément, je dirais les mêmes, le même niveau d'**études**, les mêmes **goûts**.

2 J'ai souvent besoin de petits moments où j'ai besoin d'être seul, que ce soit pour **lire**, pour **penser**, pour **écrire**, enfin toutes ces choses-là, ou tout simplement pour **être** tranquille, sans bruit, et c'est vrai que là, c'est pas toujours évident quand vous êtes dans une chambre où il y cinq ou dix personnes.

Activité 30

1 Éric est dans le même régiment que Christophe.

2 Stéphane n'a pas les mêmes goûts qu'Éric.

3 Christophe ne vient pas du même milieu social qu'Éric et Stéphane.

Activité 31

This is how your conversation should have gone:

– Alors, cela vous donne la possibilité de rencontrer des gens?

– (Yes, you meet people from different social backgrounds.)

– Oui, je rencontre des gens de milieux sociaux différents.

– Mais vous avez certainement tous le même niveau d'études?

– (Oh no. We don't necessarily have the same standard of education.)

– Oh non. On n'a pas forcément le même niveau d'études.

– Alors, si je comprends bien, il s'agit d'un mélange de milieux sociaux, de niveaux d'études et d'âges aussi peut-être?

– (Yes. That is what you like.)

– Oui. C'est ce que j'apprécie.

– Ah oui, pourquoi?

– (It's very enriching.)

– C'est très enrichissant.

Activité 32

1 J'arrive en général à comprendre la vidéo.

2 Je n'arrive pas à trouver suffisamment (*or* assez) de temps pour apprendre le vocabulaire.

3 Je n'arrive pas à prononcer le 'r'.

Here are some other possibilities:

4 J'arrive à travailler et à étudier en même temps.

5 Je n'arrive pas à me détendre le soir quand je travaille beaucoup.

Activité 33

1 J'ai besoin de regarder les informations à la télévision parce que je ne suis pas au courant du résultat des élections.

Je n'ai pas besoin de dictionnaire parce que l'ordinateur corrige automatiquement l'orthographe.

J'ai besoin d'aller à la poste parce que je n'arrive pas à trouver les timbres que j'ai achetés hier.

Je n'ai pas besoin d'argent parce que Philippe va payer pour moi.

2 Here are some of the ideas you may have had:

(a) Le week-end, j'ai besoin de tranquillité.

(b) En vacances, j'ai besoin de me détendre complètement.

(c) Au cours de la journée, j'ai besoin de trois ou quatre pauses-café.

(d) Quand je suis stressé(e), j'ai besoin de faire du yoga.

(e) Quand j'ai des problèmes, j'ai besoin de parler à mes amis.

Activité 34

Here is an example of the sort of thing you could have written:

Je vous écris/je t'écris de ma chambre à la caserne. Je la partage avec six autres appelés – Christophe, Éric, Stéphane, Olivier, Jean et François. Ils ont tous le même âge que moi. Christophe et Éric viennent d'Angers, et les autres sont de Nantes. On passe de bons moments ensemble, on plaisante, on discute, on joue au billard. La routine ici est supportable. Il faut se lever vers six heures du matin, ranger la chambre et faire sa toilette en vitesse. Ce matin, à partir de huit heures, nous avons fait l'exercice et puis j'ai eu ma première leçon de conduite.

Activité 35

1 You should have ticked (a), (c), (d), (g), (h).

2 Stéphane uses the expression *j'ai horreur de* + infinitive.

Activité 36

1 (a) (i); (b) 3; (c) 1; (d) (iii); (e) (ii); (f) (ii); (g) (ii).

2 The words written in bold indicate the changes you should have made. If you are not sure about these answers, read the video transcript to see the conscripts' actual words.

(a) Stéphane a découvert de nouveaux sports collectifs qu'il ne connaissait pas avant. **Au départ, il trouvait** le parcours d'obstacles très difficile, **mais maintenant il le fait facilement**.

(b) Christophe aime **tous les types de sport**. Ce qui est intéressant pour lui dans le parcours d'obstacles, c'est de pouvoir le faire du début jusqu'à la fin. **Il aime particulièrement** le passage de l'échelle à corde.

(c) Pour Éric, les souvenirs importants de cette petite année, ce sont les amis qu'il a connus et les bons moments qu'il a vécus, mais **aussi les permis de conduire qu'il a pu passer**.

Activité 37   You should have ticked 1, 2, 3, 5, 6, 8, 12, 15, 16.

Activité 38

1   Here are Fabien's four replies:

– Non, j'ai horreur de ça.

– Oui, c'est super.

– C'est insupportable.

– Oui, c'est très désagréable.

2   This is how the dialogue should have gone:

Mélanie	Vous aimez regarder le sport à la télévision?
Fabien	Non, j'ai horreur de ça.
Mélanie	Les vacances au bord de la mer, ça vous plaît?
Fabien	Oui, c'est super.
Mélanie	La discothèque qui est au-dessus de chez vous, qu'est-ce que vous en pensez?
Fabien	C'est insupportable.
Mélanie	Les radios sur la plage, ça vous gêne?
Fabien	Oui, c'est très désagréable.

Activité 39   En 1980 **j'ai passé** mon bac, mais **je ne l'ai pas réussi**. Il faut dire qu'à cette époque **je ne travaillais pas** beaucoup! **J'allais** tous les soirs au café avec des copains et **j'étudiais** très peu. **J'avais** dix-huit ans et pas envie de trouver un emploi. **Je ne voulais pas** continuer l'école, non plus. Les études, autrefois, **ça ne me plaisait pas** tellement. C'est à ce moment-là que **j'ai commencé** mon service militaire.

Au début, ça a été très dur, parce que **je ne connaissais** personne. Tous les jours **on faisait** des marches de vingt, vingt-cinq kilomètres, ou du parcours d'obstacles, et quand **j'étais** jeune, **je détestais** faire des efforts physiques. Et puis **ça a changé**: **j'ai fait** la connaissance de types très sympa, **j'ai pu** passer mon permis de conduire, **j'ai vécu** de vraiment bons moments. Finalement, j'ai de très bons souvenirs de mon service militaire.

Activité 40

Here is a passage of approximately 200 words, summarizing a student's experiences when starting a French course.

> Au début, je me sentais très seul(e). Je ne connaissais pas d'autres étudiants dans ma situation, mais j'étais encouragé(e) par ma famille/mes amis.
>
> Le plus difficile, c'était de trouver un moment tranquille pour regarder la vidéo et écouter les cassettes. J'avais du mal quelquefois à trouver le bon endroit sur la vidéo. Pour la prononciation, j'avais besoin de quelqu'un pour corriger mes erreurs. Je trouvais aussi qu'il était difficile de corriger les exercices. Je crois que je n'avais pas assez de confiance en moi. Le plus dur, c'était de comprendre la grammaire. Le plus difficile, c'était la différence entre le passé composé et l'imparfait.
>
> Maintenant, j'aime particulièrement la vidéo qui me donne l'impression de rencontrer beaucoup de Français de milieux différents. Ils discutent, ils racontent leur vie et j'apprends beaucoup de choses sur la société française. En général, j'arrive à comprendre la vidéo mais je dois écouter les extraits audio plusieurs fois pour bien comprendre. Et malheureusement, j'ai horreur de m'enregistrer sur la cassette. C'est utile, mais je n'aime pas du tout entendre ma voix.
>
> Je sais que j'ai fait des progrès en compréhension et j'ai appris beaucoup de nouvelles expressions. Plus j'écoute les cassettes, plus je comprends. Mais je trouve toujours qu'il est difficile d'écrire en français.

Section 3

Activité 41

1   (a) Vrai. Une coiffeuse intervient tous les quinze jours le vendredi de neuf heures à onze heures trente.

(b) Faux. Un moniteur de sport intervient le mercredi et le vendredi de quatorze heures à seize heures.

(c) Vrai. The text specifies that the *travaux manuels* are run by visitors (*animés par des visiteuses*) on Wednesday and Thursday afternoons.

(d) Faux. Une esthéticienne intervient tous les quinze jours… Une participation modique vous sera demandée (she comes once a fortnight and a small charge is made).

(e) Vrai. S'inscrire auprès des surveillantes.

(f) Faux. Il y a une séance de théâtre le jeudi, mais on ne demande pas de participation (there's a theatre workshop on Thursdays, but prisoners don't have to pay).

(g) Faux. Groupe de parole le lundi de dix-sept heures à dix-sept heures quarante-cinq.

2 (a) une comédienne

(b) un moniteur de sport

(c) une visiteuse

(d) une esthéticienne

(e) une surveillante

(f) une coiffeuse

(g) une institutrice

Activité 42

1 (a) un instituteur

(b) une monitrice de sport

2 (a) un visiteur

(b) un coiffeur

(c) un esthéticien

(d) un comédien

(e) un surveillant

3 (a) une boulangère

(b) une musicienne

(c) une chercheuse

(d) une directrice

(e) une enseignante

Activité 43

This is how the conversation should have gone:

— Excusez-moi, est-ce que vous pourriez me renseigner? Quand est-ce que je peux faire du yoga?

— Le mardi de seize heures quarante-cinq à dix-sept heures quarante-cinq.

— Et l'atelier de théâtre a lieu quand?

— Le jeudi de seize heures à dix-sept heures quarante-cinq.

— Quand est-ce que je peux faire du sport?

— Le mercredi et le vendredi de quatorze heures à seize heures.

— Et quand est-ce qu'il y a des séances d'audio-visuel?

— Le vendredi de treize heures trente à seize heures.

— Merci beaucoup.

— Je vous en prie.

Activité 44

1 The answer is *le respect*. This is what Mme Denoës says:

> Le respect. Le respect du personnel de surveillance, le respect entre détenues… tout marche bien si les personnes sont respectueuses, quoi. Nous les respectons, nous, alors en échange elles doivent aussi nous respecter.

2 Inmates would not use the *tu* form with prison officers. See explanations on *le tutoiement* (page 59) for further details.

Activité 45

1 Faux. Nicole says: *'À partir de sept heures, elles n'ont plus les clefs. C'est fini, elles ne peut plus rentrer dans nos chambres.'*

2 Vrai. She says that this is no problem: *'Autrement, dans la journée, oui, elles peuvent venir dialoguer; aucun problème'*.

3 Faux. Nicole is categorical that this is not allowed: *'Ah, non, non, non, non, non, non!... Y a pas le droit, non, non, non.'*

Activité 46

Here are some possible sentences:

1 Au Centre Pénitentiaire de Nantes, il est interdit de tutoyer les surveillantes.

2 Il faut respecter le règlement intérieur.

3 Les surveillantes ne peuvent pas prendre le café avec une détenue dans sa cellule.

4 Les détenues doivent respecter les surveillantes et vice versa.

Activité 47

Here is how the conversation should have gone:

– Pardon… est-ce que je peux garer ma voiture dans la rue ici devant l'hôtel?

– (No sir, parking is forbidden in this street.)

– Non, monsieur, le stationnement est interdit dans cette rue.

– Alors, où est-ce que je peux la garer?

– (He has to park it in the car park behind this building.)

– Il faut la garer dans le parking derrière ce bâtiment.

– Pardon, est-ce que je peux fumer ici?

– (No, it is forbidden to smoke in the lounge.)

– Non, il est interdit de fumer dans le salon.

– Alors, où est-ce que je peux fumer?

– (She is allowed to smoke in the bar.)

– Vous avez le droit de fumer au bar.

– Je pars aujourd'hui, mais est-ce que je peux rester dans la chambre jusqu'à trois heures?

– (No, he has to leave the room at midday.)

– Non, il faut quitter la chambre à midi.

– Est-ce que je peux quand même attendre en bas jusqu'à trois heures?

– (Yes, he's allowed to stay in the lounge.)

– Oui, vous avez le droit de rester dans le salon.

Activité 49

1 Faux. Nicole says: *'Tout le monde se plaint de ça'* (Everyone complains about this).

2 Vrai. She says: *'Alors donc je ne peux pas mettre ce que je voudrais; j'aimerais bien me libérer et j'ai honte; j'ai honte parce que après, quand, euh, je vois la surveillante, je, je n'aime pas...'* (She can't write what she would like to; she'd love to release her feelings, but she feels ashamed, particularly when she sees the prison officer afterwards.)

3 Faux. Nicole is asked: *'Les lettres que vous recevez sont également [lues]?'* (The letters you receive are also read?) She replies: *'Oui'*.

4 Faux. She is asked: *'Est-ce que l'on censure, c'est-à-dire est-ce que l'on vous demande de ne pas écrire certaines choses?'* She replies: *'Non, on peut écrire tout ce qu'on veut.'* (They can write anything they like – although she does go on to say that in practice she is careful about what she writes.)

5 Faux. Nicole says: *'S'il y a quelque chose qui leur semble un peu bizarre, la lettre elle doit être photocopiée et envoyée au juge'* (They are photocopied and sent to the magistrate.)

Activité 50   Here is one possible translation, but it is a guide only. Check in particular the use of tenses, shown in bold type.

> En 1993, il y **a eu** beaucoup de changements dans la Prison des Mandales. Par exemple, autrefois les surveillantes **lisaient** tout le courrier. Elles **disaient** que c'**était** pour aider les détenues, parce que chaque fois qu'une femme déprimée **parlait** de suicide dans une lettre, la surveillante le **savait** immédiatement et **pouvait** l'aider. Mais les prisonnières n'**étaient** pas contentes. Elles **trouvaient** ça insupportable. Elle **disaient** aussi que les surveillantes **étaient** trop strictes. Elles ne **parlaient** pas beaucoup aux détenues. De plus, les détenues ne **pouvaient** pas faire de sport parce qu'il n'y **avait** pas de salle de sport.

> Et puis tout **a changé** avec l'arrivée de la nouvelle directrice. Elle **a décidé** d'améliorer la vie des détenues. Elle **a organisé** des activités sportives. Il y **a eu** plus de contact entre les surveillantes et les détenues. Les femmes **ont** même **eu** le droit de voir une esthéticienne une fois par semaine.

Activité 51   1 (a) Mettre une fille au pensionnat?

- C'est une bonne chose parce qu'elle apprend la discipline. C'est vrai qu'elle peut se sentir isolée au début, mais après elle est sûre de se faire des amies durables.

- Ce n'est pas une bonne idée parce qu'elle perd tout contact avec le monde réel. C'est vrai qu'elle a plus de chances de réussir son bac, mais c'est souvent très cher.

   (You could also have put it the other way round: *parce que c'est souvent très cher* and *mais elle perd tout contact*.)

(b) Faire le service militaire?

- Ce n'est pas une bonne chose parce que les jeunes ont l'impression de perdre leur temps pendant dix mois. C'est vrai qu'ils apprennent la discipline, mais la plupart du temps ils sont obligés d'obéir à des ordres inutiles.

- C'est une bonne chose parce qu'on rencontre des gens de milieux sociaux différents. C'est vrai qu'il y a beaucoup de contraintes, mais c'est une excellente préparation à la vie professionnelle.

2 Every answer is going to be different, but here are some of the things that you might have thought of:

(a) Faut-il interdire toutes les voitures dans les centres-villes?

- C'est une bonne idée parce que les voitures sont polluantes et bruyantes. C'est vrai que la voiture est plus pratique que le bus, mais la pollution est très dangereuse pour la santé.

- Ce n'est pas une bonne idée parce que les voitures sont pratiques pour les personnes âgées et également pour les commerçants. C'est vrai qu'elles sont gênantes, mais elles sont nécessaires aussi, il faut le dire.

(b) Faut-il obliger tout le monde à apprendre une langue étrangère?

- C'est une bonne idée parce que cela facilite l'entente internationale. C'est vrai qu'apprendre une langue étrangère n'est pas toujours facile, mais il faut faire un effort.

- Ce n'est pas une bonne idée parce qu'il y a des personnes qui ne s'intéressent pas du tout aux langues étrangères. C'est vrai que cela peut être une expérience enrichissante, mais il faut aussi beaucoup de temps.

Activité 52 1(a); 2(b); 3(a).

Activité 53
1 Neither has ever had an accident at the work place.
2 The workers in Julia's workshop are not allowed to smoke.
3 Some of Julia's colleagues disagree.
4 Everybody complains about the canteen.
5 The only thing she thinks is wrong about the canteen is the quality of the food!

Activité 54
1 (a) The Service de psychiatrie provides treatment for psychological problems (*vos troubles d'ordre nerveux*) and counselling on personal problems (*vos difficultés personnelles*).
  (b) The Antenne toxicomanie provides both medical and psychological help (*un suivi médico-psychologique*) for drug addiction (*la toxicomanie*).

(c) Le Triangle d'Or also provides counselling for drug addition (*une consultation pour toxicomanes*).

(d) Le Service d'alcoologie provides counselling for all those with a drink problem (*un problème avec l'alcool*).

2   You should have given the following jobs and translations:

(a) des médecins (doctors)

(b) des psychologues (psychologists)

(c) des infirmiers/ières (male/female nurses)

(d) des psychiatres (psychiatrists)

(e) une assistante sociale (a social worker)

Activité 55

Verbes	*Noms*
prendre en charge	la prise en charge
réfléchir	une réflexion
suivre	le suivi
sortir	la sortie
s'informer	l'information
aider	l'aide
consulter	la consultation
soigner	les soins

Activité 56

1   Nicole mentions *les psychologues, les docteurs, les infirmières, les surveillantes.*

2   This is what Nicole said:

(a) Donc il y a les **psychologues** et les **docteurs**, les **infirmières**. Alors donc ils essaient, ben de **dialoguer**, de lui **donner** des **médicaments**, pour, euh… le stress, pour, euh, la déprime.

(b) Les surveillantes **sont très gentilles** parce que… elles **viennent** la **voir** en lui, en lui faisant…, en lui parlant.

Activité 57   The correct summary is 2.

Activité 58   From what we know of Nicole, the most appropriate adjectives would be:

• généreuse (generous)

• compréhensive (understanding)

• chaleureuse (warm)

Activité 59   Here is an example of the sort of thing you could have said:

Quand j'avais treize ans, ma famille est venue vivre à York. Je suis entré(e) dans un nouveau collège. Je me souviens très bien de l'établissement. C'était un énorme bâtiment en brique rouge. Il était situé dans un parc, loin du centre-ville. Je me levais le matin vers sept heures et je prenais l'autobus à huit heures quinze pour aller au collège. Le cadre était très agréable, mais les professeurs n'étaient pas très motivants et ne s'intéressaient pas du tout à nos problèmes. Ils n'arrivaient pas à faire respecter les règles du collège et en général, pendant les cours, les élèves faisaient beaucoup de bruit. Je détestais ce collège. J'avais horreur des cours de géographie, mais j'aimais bien les cours d'histoire. Avec le professeur d'histoire, on faisait beaucoup de sorties. Par exemple, nous sommes allé(e)s deux fois au musée archéologique de York. J'aimais aussi les activités sportives et je participais souvent à des concours de tennis.

En 1980, j'ai réussi à mes examens et j'ai décidé de suivre une formation d'ingénieur. En 1983, j'ai eu mon diplôme d'ingénieur et j'ai trouvé un travail dans la région de York. Je dois beaucoup voyager et ce travail me plaît énormément.

Acknowledgements

Grateful acknowledgement is made to the following sources for permission to reproduce material in this book:

p. 13: courtesy of Institution Blanche de Castille: p. 31: extracts from *Le Quid*, 1990, courtesy of Éditions Robert Laffont; p. 33: *Service national, vous et nous, un service à se rendre*, no. 98, September 1993, courtesy of ADDIM, Paris; pp. 55, 66: *Bulletin arivant*, Ministère de la Justice, Nantes.

Drawings p. 46 by Gary Rees. Cover photograph by David Sheppard.

This book is part of L120 *Ouverture: a fresh start in French.*

Cadences

1   L'année mode d'emploi

2   Le temps libre et le temps plein

3   Vivre en collectivité

4   Vivre la nuit

Valeurs

1   Marketing et consommation

2   Gagner sa vie

3   Douce France?

4   La qualité de la vie

The two parts of the course are also sold separately as packs.

L500 *Cadences: update your French*

L501 *Valeurs: moving on in French*